PENGUIN BOOKS AND BLUE SALT
THE BAD BOYS OF BOKARO JAIL

Chetan Mahajan is the CEO of HCL Learning Ltd. He has lived for many years in the US, where he earned an MBA from the Kellogg School of Management. He now lives with his family in Delhi NCR.

Blue Salt is an imprint dedicated to noir and crime, established by the bestselling writer S. Hussain Zaidi and co-published by Penguin.

THE BAD BOYS OF BOKARO JAIL

CHETAN MAHAJAN

BLUE
SALT

PENGUIN BOOKS

PENGUIN BOOKS
Published by the Penguin Group
Penguin Books India Pvt. Ltd, 11 Community Centre, Panchsheel Park,
New Delhi 110 017, India
Penguin Group (USA) Inc., 375 Hudson Street, New York, New York 10014, USA
Penguin Group (Canada), 90 Eglinton Avenue East, Suite 700, Toronto, Ontario,
M4P 2Y3, Canada (a division of Pearson Penguin Canada Inc.)
Penguin Books Ltd, 80 Strand, London WC2R 0RL, England
Penguin Ireland, 25 St Stephen's Green, Dublin 2, Ireland (a division of Penguin Books Ltd)
Penguin Group (Australia), 707 Collins Street, Melbourne, Victoria 3008, Australia
(a division of Pearson Australia Group Pty Ltd)
Penguin Group (NZ), 67 Apollo Drive, Rosedale, Auckland 0632, New Zealand
(a division of Pearson New Zealand Ltd)
Penguin Books (South Africa) (Pty) Ltd, Block D, Rosebank Office Park, 181 Jan Smuts
Avenue, Parktown North, Johannesburg 2193, South Africa

Penguin Books Ltd, Registered Offices: 80 Strand, London WC2R 0RL, England

First published by Penguin Books India and Blue Salt 2014

Copyright © Chetan Mahajan 2014

10 9 8 7 6 5 4 3 2 1

ISBN 9780143421535

Typeset in Adobe Garamond by SÜRYA, New Delhi
Printed at Thomson Press India Ltd, New Delhi

Dedicated to family and friends, who demonstrated incredible strength and faith, and most especially to my father who was there when I needed him

LAYOUT OF BOKARO JAIL

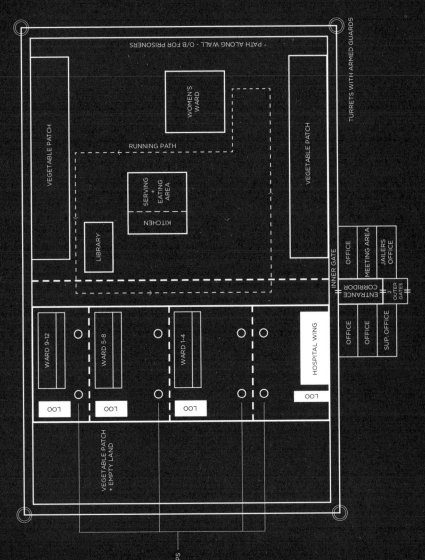

Prologue

SMS sent to an IAS officer friend:

24 Dec, 6.03 a.m.

> Hi Vatsala. This is Chetan Mahajan. I am in a spot since yesterday noon. Spent the night at the police station. All explained below. Can you help? Thanks!! I am an employee of Everonn—a listed company. Joined Oct 3 this year. We run an IIT coaching centre in Bokaro. Some faculty here quit and moved to another company. Because of that parents have asked for a refund which I am unable to give instantly. The police (P.S. Sector 4 Bokaro) is detaining me forcibly and not allowing me to leave. Since I am only an employee not sure this is legal. Appreciate any help so that police releases me. Thanks. Chetan Mahajan

SMS exchange with company MD:

23 Dec, 8.00 p.m.

> Situation out of hand. Detained at the police station and forced to spend the night here. Trust someone can reach here early tmrw to help sort things out and implement refund. Tks.

23 Dec, 8.10 p.m.

> I had a message that u would be out by now . . .

1

23 Dec, 8.15 p.m.

Still here and no such hope so far

24 Dec, 6.47 a.m.

Rakesh, if the FIR is filed today and I am arrested
(even if later it is established as wrong) the earliest
opportunity to post bail would be Jan 4 because of
courts being closed until then. Tks.

24 Dec, 9.16 a.m.

Hi Rakesh, Any update on the letter? Parents have
started arriving and I need the letter pacifying
parents urgently. Please email it. Tks.

24 Dec, 9.17 a.m.

I m out at the moment and not in office. I Hv
asked it to be drafted . . .

24 Dec. 9.18 a.m.

Please CC me.

24 Dec, 9.19 a.m.

Noted. I may ask company secretary to sign
and put Company seal

24 Dec, 9.21 a.m.

I think your name and Title of MD
being on it is critical

24 Dec, 9.22 a.m.

OK. Will work out . . .

24 Dec, 9.24 a.m.

Who should it b addressed to

24 Dec, 9.24 a.m.

Parents and students of Toppers Bokaro

24 Dec, 9.25 a.m.

That will mean a blanket to all parents. U ok with that . . .

24 Dec, 12.13 p.m.

Person left for SBI Perungudi for cash deposit: 30 K * 13. 4 students in other bank not having IFSC Code, cash will be deposited.Balance 7 students will be transferred by NEFT. Will arrange the scan copy of proof at the earliest. Regards.

24 Dec, 12.20 p.m.

Great. Thanks!

24 Dec, 2.09 p.m.

Deposit proof of all 24 refunds emailed to u

24 Dec, 2.22 p.m.

Thanks

24 Dec, 3.23 p.m.

Pls keep me posted on 2nd list of refunds being processed. Treat with same urgency as first. Thanks!

24 Dec, 3.23 p.m.

Ok

24 Dec, 3.53 p.m.

We have completed NEFT Request for all 24 student of list 2 and balance of list 1. Our Person is on the way to the bank. Transfer should b done today and expected acknowledgement in next 2 hours. Regards.

24 Dec, 3.59 p.m.

Going to jail. Please take all calls from Vandita, my wife

A few people had told me that I had 'arrived in life'. Soon after that, I arrived in jail. This is the story of the time I spent imprisoned in the Bokaro Jail. I wrote this daily account while inside jail. All the information here is factual and the experiences related are all true. Only some names have been changed.

23 December 2012

By definition, I guess I am an overgrown yuppie. 42 years old. Two MBAs: one from India and one from the US. Lived in the US for seven years. Big house in a big city, working for a listed company for a hefty salary. Gorgeous, highly educated wife. Two amazingly cute, loving kids. Two dogs. Two cars.

Today I have been taken to the police station and detained for 24 hours. The accusation is one of fraud (sections 420, 406 and 34) against Everonn, my employer whom I joined less than three months ago. Being the seniormost employee physically present I am the one who has been arrested. And why was I arrested? Well, we (my employer and I) are in the education business, and we have an IIT entrance coaching chain called 'Toppers' which has a strong presence in Bokaro City. However, it has been short of funds and compromises have been made in the quality of what we deliver. A few of our employees have defected to competition without any intimation to us. We arranged for continuation of services very quickly with manpower we had sourced from elsewhere. My visit to Bokaro was supposed to be a short two-day affair to reassure our customers that nothing has changed and that all our commitments would be met.

What I did not know is that a couple of similar businesses in the same line of work have shut down in the past two years, and many of those customers lost all their money. I had one session with our customers on day one (22 December) and that went okay. But today a few customers (parents) became adamant and demanded an instant refund. With the earlier shutdowns in the background, they are not willing to take anyone's word on anything. However, a refund decision is not one I can take independently. Today is a Sunday and my superiors in the company are hard to reach. Even with the required approvals, there is no way I can arrange such refunds instantly. Not satisfied with my response, the parents call the police. The cops arrive with a very clear assumption of 'guilty until proven innocent'. In fact SHO Surinder Singh himself makes a statement—that, too, in front of all the parents—that our institute would be shut down. That does not help.

A few parents file a police complaint. I am taken from the office to the police station. The SHO tells me I have 24 hours to pacify the customers (students and their parents) or I will be arrested. During these 24 hours I cannot leave the police station. No papers are shown to me. No rights read out. No grounds for the detention are given.

I repeatedly explain that I am just an employee, and

that I had recently joined the company. Neither have I collected any money, nor am I authorized to distribute it. But all my pleas mean nothing. Someone needs to be hung, and I am conveniently available.

This was a situation I had not even dreamed of two days ago. I had joined Everonn on 3 October with stars in my eyes. I was being brought in to run virtually half the company. The company itself was going through a bad patch. The founder and erstwhile CEO had been arrested for tax evasion and imprisoned over one year back, and ever since then the whole company seems to have been coming apart. Then late last year the Gems group of Dubai—a large conglomerate from the Middle East that owns a very successful chain of schools there—had bought the company, and effectively taken control. However, while they had bought the company, they had left the old management in control, and so while the company now had access to funds it still had not changed to become a well-run, profitable business. Almost a year had gone by, but nothing substantial had changed on the ground. It was only in September that they finally seemed to have realized that a change in results would require a new leadership. To bring about this change they had brought on board one of the most respected professionals of the education industry as an advisor. This gentleman knew me well, and had reached out to me to be part of the new leadership at the company.

The scenario laid out before me was challenging, but also had a lot of potential. A company with many different divisions and businesses going through rough times. A new, professional management team, which was well funded and had good intent. And a free hand for me to evaluate the various businesses in my division, and choose the businesses to focus upon and build and which ones to exit. I had joined with the plan of building something substantial and valuable which I could be proud of. It was a great next step in my career. I had worked in vocational education and school education, run start-ups, sold e-learning and also been an investor in the education industry—both in India and the US. This job was an opportunity to use all my skills, experience and industry knowledge to breathe life back into a once-strong but now struggling brand.

The first two months had been frustrating, and also rewarding. The team was really demotivated, but there were pockets of talent and passion. We struggled with the cash situation as working capital was always short. Against all odds we had just won a large project bid for a big corporate to provide e-learning services. Talent was leaving very rapidly but some businesses and brands were truly strong in their own pockets. 'Toppers' in Bokaro was one of the strongest businesses left in Everonn. I had every intention of building it and making it even stronger.

But all that strategic thinking is a distant dream now. The reality of today is to do what it takes to stay out of jail. Hours are spent on frantic phone calls and SMSs trying to figure out how to arrange funds and ensure that payments can be made on priority, and over a weekend. People work through Sunday and we arrive at some idea of how much money is readily available and can be refunded. The liquidity situation is bad and to refund 600 parents in one shot is literally impossible.

Some twenty-four parents of our students are at the police station, and I try and work out an arrangement where I promise them that we will refund them first thing when the banks open on Monday morning. In return these parents would need to convince all the other parents that we are honourable and have every intention of refunding everybody. In hindsight, it was pretty hopeless. The parents not refunded had little basis to believe the company, or another parent who had already received a refund.

24 December 2012

Today I am arrested and put in jail. The papers carry my photograph leaving our Bokaro office with the police.

The stories in the media, just like the police, have assumed that we are guilty until proven innocent. In fact, the *Dainik Jagaran* newspaper quotes the SP, Kuldip Dwivedi, saying that our institute has been shut after we have taken money from the students—which is complete bullshit. I guess it helps sell a few more copies of the *Dainik Jagaran*, though. Today we finally do almost fifty refunds. It is not enough. The whole town knows of the story and of my presence at the police station. Hundreds of parents and students turn up claiming refunds. I stay inside the station but the noise from outside is frightening. Every once in a while a cop shouts at the crowd in an effort at crowd control. Everyone wants their money back instantly. So the list of the refund requests goes from 24 in the first list to fifty by the second list to a total of over 600 by noon. Over 600 customers, wanting instant refunds.

The deadline for me to convince the parents—4 p.m.— is fast approaching. Everonn has identified a lawyer who also arrives at the police station, but isn't able to change anything much. At 4 p.m the hordes of parents outside are at their angry best. The police asks me to sign an official set of documents. Again nobody explains anything. I am put in the jeep and sent off. I realize that I have just been arrested and am going to jail.

I am not handcuffed as I am put in the jeep. After leaving the police station, the first stop is for the medical check-up. In the jeep are four policemen. Two in front and two in the backseat where I am sitting—one on either side of me. They are all curious about the case against me, and ask me the details. As they hear the story and also converse more with me, they start treating me a little more deferentially as I probably sound more educated and am better dressed than the average joe they arrest. At the hospital which we reach for the check-up they apologetically say they would have to handcuff me before I get off. A handcuff is produced, and my wrist along with a thick rope is put in a single ring, squeezing my wrist a little. The rope is held by the cop and I am led into the hospital.

The medical check-up is a complete sham. The doctor asks my age and if I have any medical problems. He also asks if I had been beaten or manhandled. I say no to both questions, and we are done. I desperately need to pee, and tell the cop. Instead of taking me to a toilet, which the hospital presumably would have, he says 'Baahar kar leejiye' (Do it outside). With that he leads me down the road, and

I pee into the bushes, still on my leash. It helps me empathize with Cleo, my pet Doberman.

After another stop at the court we head to the house of the magistrate. Evidently 5 p.m. is too late for them to be in office. Since the magistrate is clearly an educated man, I tell him again that I have recently joined this company, and ask if there is any way for me to stay out of jail. He simply tells me that other company officials are also named in the FIR, but that I would have to go to jail. By the time we are back in the jeep it is turning dark.

I am shit-scared. I have barely ever even been to a police station, leave alone a jail. I borrow a phone (I have given mine to the lawyer along with all my other stuff) from one of the cops and speak to Vandita, my wife. I tell her that I love her and that she has to do everything to get me out. And that I do not deserve this. Sitting in the police jeep, travelling through the night surrounded by the four policemen, I cry.

The images playing in my head are scary. Am I going to be alone in a cell? Or would I share it with one or two criminals? Would I get to see the sun? Talk to people? Would there be bedbugs? Cockroaches? Centipedes? Would I be beaten? Raped?

When we finally reach the jail it is night. The jail is an imposing structure. Like all jails, I guess. High walls stretching out on both sides. Watchtower silhouettes in the distance. A glint of torchlight bouncing off gunmetal in the turret. The jeep stops outside and we walk to a huge metal gate large enough to let in a vehicle. The smaller, man-sized door in the gate needs two people to open it: one person to unlock the huge padlock on the outside, and another on the inside. This gate is opened, and there is a similar second gate inside. That is also opened and I am led into Bokaro Chas Mandal Karawas, the Bokaro-Chas Jail, in my Ralph Lauren jacket and my Aldo shoes.

The inner gate opens into a wide corridor with a third gate of equal size at the far end. Many doors open into the corridor on both sides. All seem locked. A short, pudgy policeman stands in the corridor along with another man in a track-suit.

Once we are safely inside and the padlocks are in place again and secure, the cop from the jeep finally takes off the handcuffs, completes some paperwork, and leaves. The cop inside then starts asking me questions. He is short—maybe 5 feet 3 inches, with a substantial girth. He somehow reminds me of a goldfish. Puffy cheeks, greedy eyes. His small moustache is just a tad longer than Hitler's.

First he asks me to tell him what all I am carrying. I have just the clothes I am in. Not expecting ever to actually be arrested I have not packed—not that I would have known what to pack! I just have some random stuff—wallet with some cash, pen, card holder etc. The cash in my wallet is the only thing interesting to the cop. He looks me up and down making a bit of a show of it, and says 'He should go to the hospital ward.'

The other guy in the track-suit nods. I am very fit and

healthy, so I don't really know why I need to be in the hospital ward, but do not say anything. I guess things will play themselves out.

'So what should we do about the money?' The cop asks, no one in particular.

Silence for a bit. He fingers the card-holder and handkerchief on the table.

'Can I take it inside?' I ask. I have no idea if I would need cash inside.

'It is not allowed,' he says. 'But you should go to the hospital ward.'

I still wasn't sure if I wanted to go to the hospital ward or not, but this cop makes it sound really cool and aspirational. Tacit wink-wink nudge-nudge type signals, but nothing is spoken. Maybe I am just imagining things?

'So what should we do with the money?' he asks yet again.

'I guess you can keep some and give me the rest,' I say. Maybe I am bribing him to get me into the hospital ward. Maybe I am not.

'How much?' he asks, pointing to the wallet.

'Give me some 2 or 3 hundred,' I say. He keeps 800 and gives me the balance of 270 which I innocently put in my hip pocket.

The two of them then make a list of all my remaining stuff, and one copy of the list. We go through one of the side doors of the corridor into an office. They put all the stuff and one copy of the list in an envelope, seal it and lock it in a cupboard inside the office. We then come back into the corridor and head to the inner gate. Fishface calls out and a cop appears on the other side. Heavy padlocks are unlocked on both sides, and I walk out of the corridor into a scary, unknown darkness. A policeman with a stick escorts me. As the gate opens a strong torch beam is focused on me and my escort. We walked down a long, straight and dark path lit only by the torch beam we are walking towards. No moon visible. Not a word is spoken. Finally we reach a building where two cops are sitting.

I realize I am alone inside a Jharkhand jail with three cops, all carrying sticks. It is pitch black. I am miles away from anything. If they started to hit me or beat me up or rape and fuck me I could scream my guts out and nobody would come to my rescue. I try not to dwell on that thought.

These policemen again ask the same set of standard questions which I have come to expect within just a few hours of dealing with policemen—at the police station, in the police jeep, and now in jail.

'*Kya case main aaye ho?*' (What case are you in for?)

Initially my answer is 'fraud' but that is too much English and the response quickly became '*Chaar-sau-beesi*' (a case under section 420).

'*Kitney ka ghotala hai?*' (What is the amount of money involved?)

Initially, my response is fuzzy again as I actually do not know the specific amount. How many customers/what

15

amount of refunds etc. Again, it does not work. These guys needed a number to hang their hat on. So I quickly settle on 20–30 lakh rupees.

A natural corollary of this conversation is my explaining how I am just an employee and have not taken the 20–30 lakhs home with me. How I joined the company less than three months ago.

One other question which everyone asks without hesitation is 'How much do you make?'

'You mean salary?' I ask. Where I come from, that would be considered a very personal question, if not a rude one.

Nod from the cop.

This is a tricky one. In fact this question was asked yesterday by the SHO at the police station. My response there had been a number much lower than my actual income. The SHO's response was a guffaw and a quick question to the *sipahi* (policeman) standing there asking him how many years he would take to make that much.

My 'high' income probably made him want to arrest me even more.

Lesson learnt, the number I now mention to the cop in the jail goes down as acceptable. As this Q&A goes on, another prisoner is brought in by the guard. Thin young man. Unkempt hair. Dirty uneven teeth with one front tooth missing.

The cop asks him why he is in. He says he was carrying some metal rods and the police accused him of having stolen them so they had arrested him. The cop looks carefully at him.

'You've been here before.'

Not a question. A statement.

Sheepishly the man says yes. Probably a petty criminal. The cop goes on to check the man's bag. This guy knows the drill, and had packed for jail. A plastic bag with a rather dirty change of clothes, a *gamchha* (a thin towel), comb, some personal effects.

The cop then searches him thoroughly, finds nothing, and shifts his focus to me. He frisks me quite thoroughly, and makes me remove my shoes. He looks very carefully at the pen and two business cards I have in my coat pocket. I have kept them just in case I wanted to write something down. Finally hands them back. He then finds the 270 rupees fish-face returned to me in my hip pocket. Looks at me, looks at the money. He then hands it to the other cop who puts it in his pocket. Not a word is spoken. No explanations offered. No jail policy. No reprimand.

They start discussing which ward I should be sent to. I mention something about being in the hospital ward, which is completely ignored by the cops. They then say we both need to go to Ward 2. Once we are done with the search the topic changes. They ask me about my background and then the cop starts seeking career advice for his son, who is in high school. Since I am in the education industry, he figures I am some kind of expert. Evidently his son is academically quite strong and our man has him going to a coaching institute (one of our competitors) and wants my inputs on the better engineering colleges etc. I am happy to oblige. The conversation is casual and pleasant, as though the person who took my money from me is someone else.

The cop escorts me and the other late entrant to Ward 2. He runs his *danda* (stick) along the metal bars of the window, and a bearded face with a proud, upturned moustache appears behind the thick iron bars. Brief conversation, and then the cop unlocks the heavy padlock on the door and we are inside Ward 2.

The door clangs shut behind us, and we walk into a large room—some 20 feet by 70 feet in size. Two bare light bulbs are lit at either end—not nearly enough light for a room this size. Some 25 men are inside. Many sitting in groups playing cards. Some talking idly. One group in the far corner looks like a set of particularly heavy-set men. Or maybe they're just wearing extra clothing to keep warm. I hope.

The bearded guy motions for us to sit on a thin blanket spread on the floor. I can sense a lot of curious eyes upon us—especially me. The bearded guy's name is Vijay, and he asks us if we have eaten. That is when I realize I have eaten nothing all day. It has been such a busy, stressful day that I have not even thought of food.

I look around the room more carefully. It is a strange room. The Indian tricolour is painted along three walls, punctuated by windows with ultra-thick iron bars, and also by clothes hanging from thin ropes along the walls. One wall is a huge mural of Ganesh and Parvati. At least I think it is Parvati—I am not so good with my gods. A small area, about five feet from that particular wall, is cordoned off with a curtain strung about one foot off the ground as the 'Temple' or 'God' end of the cell. Blankets or other makeshift mattresses covered with sheets line half the room, with a path down the middle leading to the temple. At the other end of the room is a small door to one side—presumably the loo. Also a lone mattress at the other corner of the room has a few men on it. Some smoke is rising from that corner. It vaguely gives the feel of an opium den. Though I've never been in one, this is what I imagine it would be like. Appropriate in the non-God end of the cell.

Ironic that both ends give off smoke—just at different times of the day.

There is this young boy walking up and down the ward—probably no older than 17—who is generally making comments and joking around with the prisoners in the ward. He is a lean, good-looking, cheerful kid who makes the otherwise dark ward a little brighter and livelier. Not knowing his name I just think of him as 'Bouncy Boy'.

Most of the men continue with whatever they are doing, although I still notice the occasional curious glance. In a bit a couple of them come over and start asking questions:

'*Kaun case mein aaye ho?*' (What case are you in for?)

'*Chaar-sau-beesi ka case hai*' (The case is under section 420) I reply.

'*Kaun thaane se?*' (From which police station?)

'Sector four police station'

'SHO Surinder Singh,' one says to the other knowingly.

'*Bahut maarta hai maader-chod*' (The motherfucker really beats a lot.)

An exchange of stories follows with the prisoners comparing notes on how much Surinder Singh had beaten them.

. . . 'How much money is involved?' . . . 'How much does the company pay you? . . .'

The conversation soon turns to advice. Amongst the men who talk to me are a couple of relatively educated sounding men. They say 'In the jail it's all about money. Everything is available for a price. Normally you have to stand in line like an animal to even get your food, do lots of physical labour etc. In this ward—Ward 2—you don't have to do anything. No labour or standing in line for food. Also, the food is better, and collected by other people and kept for you. The food is served to you at decent hours, and nobody harasses you. You are safe. We have been here for a month, and we like it here.'

'So how does one get to stay here in Ward 2?' I ask.

'You talk to Ghani Bhai.'

'Who?' I ask.

'Ghani Bhai. Ghani Ansari. Sitting in the corner there.'

He points to the smoke-encircled, lone mattress in the far end. The ungodly end.

As the conversation goes deeper they explain that everyone has to, of course, pay to enjoy such privileges. They say that it had cost them ten thousand rupees. A guy named Dharmendar who is sitting on the next mattress jumps in and also starts talking about the ward and its benefits etc. He says that to stay in the ward one has to pay 10,000 rupees as a one-time expense.

Just then Vijay announces that dinner is ready. Some sack-cloth mats are laid out around a stack of pots, and some plates are handed out. Five or six of us sit facing the pots and pans and Vijay dishes out some food to one row of prisoners. All the food is cold. The vegetable curry from the prison kitchen—a soupy broth with bits of vegetable— looks really unappetizing. The dal is a cold, thin yellow soup. My two new 'friends'—their names are Vinod and Shant—sit next to me, and insist that I share their food. Evidently they had '*mulakatis*' (jailspeak for visitors) that morning who had brought home-made food. Five stuffed parathas are plonked in my plate. I thank them and give one back. Some sabzi from the jail's supply is also served and I go to work. Man, am I hungry! Home-made parathas as my first meal in jail. I am not complaining.

A dirty-yellow plastic bottle with water in it is put before us. No glasses. Vinod and Shant pick up the bottle and drink. Nobody touches the bottle to their mouth, but they drink heartily. Typically, when I travel I drink bottled water. No clue how clean that bottle is inside but from the outside it is filthy. But I have no choice.

I pick up the bottle and drink.

After dinner I go across to the corner where Ghani Bhai is supposed to be sitting. I am not sure which one he is but as I approach, a dark man waves to me to sit next to him. He is lean, dark and has a moustache. Probably mid-30s. His teeth are stained yellow and he has high cheekbones and a clean look—like one of the porters from *Tintin in Tibet*. He is soft-spoken and brief, but not unpleasant.

'So you have understood how it works here?' Ghani Bhai asks.

'Yes, Dharmendar explained it to me,' I say, pointing to Dharmendar, who has sat down next to me.

Ghani briefly repeats the information: safety, no work etc. But he ends by saying that I should never talk about money to anyone. I am not to step outside the ward for the next day or two. If I have to, I am not to talk to anyone. And if anyone asks who I am or where I am from, I should simply say that I knew Dharmendar from earlier, and I am from his hometown—Jahanabad. I am not to tell people that I am from Delhi or from out of town. I am to say that I live in Bokaro, in sector four or some such. Dharmendar nods in agreement at various points.

After having briefed me, Ghani turns to his dinner. He is sitting on the mattress and next to him on the floor is a thali with a massive stack of rotis and some sabzi. As he starts to eat, Bouncy Boy plonks himself down across from Ghani Bhai. Two small steel lunch-boxes are opened—one has dal from the jail supply, and the other contains *palak-paneer*—obviously from some outside source. It certainly had not been part of the meal served by Vijay. It does not look much like jail food. The kid slowly stirs the dal with his finger to make it uniformly consistent, and then he and Ghani proceed to demolish the food.

While they eat, Ghani's coterie re-runs me through the benefits of Ward 2.

'In other wards they torture you'.

'They will make you sweep the floor and clean toilets.'

'The other wards have dangerous criminals. This one is safer.'

After a bit of this I make a motion as if to leave, but Ghani gestures that I should stay. After he finishes his dinner he lets out a loud belch, washes his hands in his plate, and asks, 'So you understand? It is okay, right?'

'Yes, but I have no money,' I say.

'Tell your visitors when they come that they need to bring cash. If you come through the gate with money the cops will keep 20 per cent. If you let me know in advance I can arrange for it to be brought in cheaper. You can pay me in 2-3 days.'

Bokaro is a long way from my family, which is in Delhi. I really have no way of knowing when I will have visitors.

'I am not sure when I will have visitors. It may take more than 2-3 days.'

'Okay, you have a week. But remember I have to arrange to pay-off various people in the system to arrange all this. So even if you go somewhere else in four days you still need to pay.'

Okay, I nod. But I am not sure exactly what I am signing up for. Everyone who is advising me that Ward 2 is the best lives in that ward. I do not know whom to trust—all these people are complete strangers. I am not too sure of the motives behind all the advice. As I look around, this place isn't exactly the lap of luxury. Everyone sleeps on the floor—only hard mattresses of indeterminate warmth separate you from the cold stone. The cell is so badly lit that it would be near impossible to read anything here after dark. It is clean enough, and though the bathroom door opens into the room it doesn't smell so bad—which cannot be said for the breath of some of my fellow prisoners.

However, my immediate concern is one of safety not comfort. And no, I certainly do not want to be cleaning bathrooms or digging ditches or something. Anyway, I have verbally agreed now and I am not sure if going back on that would be easy in here. It is done.

I am allotted a mattress next to Dharmendar. I pick up two blankets from a big stack against a wall. I have been wearing the clothes I am in for two days now. I hang my coat and lie down to sleep. I haven't slept in a room with 25 other men since I was a teenager. And while I am a little more comfortable after my chat with Shant and

Vinod, and later Ghani, I still would not use the word 'safe' to describe how I felt. After all, I had to spend the entire night here.

Had I been feeling stronger and fresher maybe the apprehension would have kept me awake. But I am dog-tired and have just had my only meal of the day—and a really big one at that. I wrap myself in my blankets, lie down and quickly drift off to sleep in the same clothes yet again.

It is a noisy night. The belching and burping which started at dinnertime continues well into the night. There is a particular satisfaction that the Jharkhand man derives from belching as loudly and visibly as possible. As more and more people move to their beds, the belching is replaced by snoring. And as morning approaches farting also joins the chorus. Everyone sleeps with their heads next to the passage down the middle of the room, their feet towards the walls. Every once in a while someone would thump by my head walking towards the loo, and thump right back two or three minutes later.

Had I not been so tired—and well fed after so long—I would probably not have slept much. But while all the night sounds do register, I still get a decent night's sleep.

25 December 2012

Merry Christmas!!

6.30 p.m. I hear loud calls of the word *'jora'* (pairs): first from a cop outside and then repeated by some of the prisoners in the ward. I am asked—with a certain sense of urgency—to sit up facing another prisoner. The ward door is unlocked and a cop walks in, swinging his stick. He counts the number of pairs, makes a note, and leaves the cell door open.

Cold air comes in. I just want to stay curled up in my blanket. A huge part of me wishes I will wake up from a terrible nightmare. My mattress on the floor and blankets are cosy but not comfortable. I have my socks on to keep me warm—shoes are not allowed inside the cell, and have been left outside. And the windowsill next to the loo is stacked with shoes kept there for safekeeping from theft. In a while I get out of 'bed' and decide to take a look around so I put on my shoes and step outside. The outside area is as dirty as the room itself is clean. People spit everywhere, and trash is thrown about in most corners and along the walls. At the far end, a section of the wall has been converted into a public urinal.

However, the place is green and has a fair share of trees. There are pigeons being fed pieces of rotis by a prisoner. Some birdsong can be heard. As I walk around, the layout of the jail becomes apparent. There are three double-storey buildings, each housing four wards—two each on the ground and first floor. There is a separate boundary wall and gate for each building. Each gate opens into a larger, common courtyard which has some trees and paths. I realize that the path I had walked down yesterday, in the dark, is actually lined with rose bushes, many of which are in full bloom. And the building in the veranda of which the cop had frisked me had a signboard saying 'Library'. In the middle of the courtyard is a large room with a sloping tin roof, which is the jail kitchen.

As I walk around, I start to feel a lot of curious eyes on me. Strangers walk up and start asking questions so I head back inside. At about 7.30 a.m. an announcement is made over the PA system. '*Subah ka chai file mein chalaya ja raha hai. Bandi kripya apna chai le lein.*' (Morning tea is being is being served on the file. All prisoners please collect your tea). Not quite sure what 'file' meant I asked some of my fellow inmates who simply said it was the place where food was served. Once upon a time it may have meant 'single file' in English but it had turned into jail jargon now.

As I start to head out, one of the ward men motions for me to stay put. Tea is brought into the ward. One of the inmates takes a sip, spits it out, and says

'*Bakri ka moot hai sala*' (It's bloody goat-piss).

At my home, morning tea is a daily habit with us. We have tea in large mugs with lots of ginger, lightly brewed, certainly not over-boiled. Typically, we have it with rusks. Here, I am handed a steel glass with some brownish-yellow liquid. Steam is rising from it. Hesitantly I take a sip of the pale decoction and am tempted to spit it out myself. The only reason to drink the stuff is that it is hot. But then in a while a 'special tea' is brought around for a select few. I am handed a tiny cup, but it contains some more recognizable, super-sweet tea.

The jail is not exactly serene. There are men milling around all the time. You can hear people calling out to each other, and loud conversations go on pretty much perpetually. The noise of the handpumps, and the clang of metal buckets or improvised plastic buckets (which all started life as branded buckets of paint) add to the din.

The rest of the morning Ghani and his crew spend being super-nice to me. As the sun rises higher, I am invited to join Ghani outside on a sack-cloth rug spread out in a sunny spot at the side of the building. A glass full of sattu is handed to me. Sattu is a powder made of ground chick-peas. It is also served as a drink after mixing in water, and spicing it up with some salt, onions etc., and the drink goes by the same name. Just for a moment I wonder what water it has been made with—I know sattu is not heated or boiled—but then I give up on that thought. Pointless.

The sattu is heavy and rather too salty, but I am not turning anything half-decent away—God knows what the next meal will be like. I finish it and feel quite full: it is really heavy. Couldn't have had more. As I finish the sattu, Ghani and his boys chat about whether the one remaining glass of the drink would be enough for the 'Zamindar' or if they would need to make some more. Evidently the previous day he had had three glasses!

I am advised yet again by Ghani's sycophants not to wander around or talk to any strangers, and again not to tell anyone that I came from Delhi. 'Men can be sold like cattle in here.' I am not very clear what that means but have little desire to find out first-hand. And in some corner of my mind I feel like cattle already: haven't I already agreed to a price for the ward?

As we sit there, the warm winter sun feels nice. The newspaper arrives. It is the popular Hindi daily's city edition. The story of my arrest is on the front page: headline news, competing with the coverage of the Delhi gang rape story. A young man, also from Ward 2 sits next to me. He reads the gang rape story aloud for a bit and says, 'There is no way I am getting bail now.'

I can only guess his crime but do not ask.

The newspaper quickly disintegrates into many separate sheets that many of the prisoners read simultaneously. There is a lot of interest in my story—especially in how much money was swindled. Different papers give different numbers but the general consensus within the jail is two crore. Again a series of questions are showered on me, and again I repeat my story. Employee . . . just joined . . . etc.

In a while I brush my teeth, except that I don't have a toothbrush. First I attempt brushing using my finger as a brush with some donated toothpaste. That doesn't work too well so I try the *daatun*—twigs from a local tree called sakhua. This is one thing freely available in the jail. The daatun is hard but once I chew it for a while it softens and forms into bristles. Much better toothbrush than my finger.

The toilet facilities are basic, and rather dirty. There is a common set of toilets outside shared by all the four wards within one building compound—the toilet inside the cell is cleaner. But it is supposed to be used only during lock-up time.

The water for all purposes comes from handpumps, of which there are two in each compound. I realize that a handpump is the ultimate water-saving device as nobody unnecessarily pumps more than they need.

Given my 'special' status—let's see how long that lasts— I am provided with a bucket of water. There is no bathroom to bathe in—everyone bathes in the open in their undies, with cold water freshly drawn from the handpump. However, if the water is freshly pumped it is somewhat warm, and if one bathes in the sun it isn't that bad. Since I have no towel, one of my ward-mates named Jabra generously offers to lend me his gamchha (thin cloth which also acts as a towel). Jabra is one of Ghani's lieutenants. He has long hair, a beard, a slight limp and he enjoys singing. And he sings really well—I heard him briefly that morning as he sang to himself. The gamchha is dirty and tattered, but it is either that or no bath third day in a row. And while borrowing a towel is a big deal for me, it clearly isn't for anyone else. The place where I am to take a bath is a sunny spot at the back of the ward building. It is supposed to be a special privilege that someone has filled in water and brought it to this sunny spot—all handpumps are in the shade. There are a few broken pieces of concrete next to the wall where the bucket of water is placed.

As I take my bath, Jabra stands watch over me. Halfway through he says, 'Why don't you stand on the slab and bathe?' I am wondering what he is talking about. Helpfully, he points to the assortment of concrete pieces. Seems a bit of a balancing act, but it is better than being in the mud. I try and complete the rest of my bath on the 'slab'. Then I get back into the same clothes for the third day sans my undies—which are beyond recycling—and await what comes next.

Ward 2 is full of interesting characters. There is Dharmendar, the good-looking and rather well-built lieutenant of Ghani. There is Jabra, the singer with his perpetual dour look, but again one of the men about town. Then, of course, there is Ghani himself. A bit of an enigma, but I have overheard people in the jail say that he likes it inside the jail but is miserable when outside. Then there is Bouncy Boy, walking around the ward in his John Travolta gait chiding one person and messing with someone else's hair, with a perpetual smile on his face.

Everyone in the entire jail seems loud, except Ghani. I guess in these parts it is just normal to be loud. Everyone is also very full of bravado—making tall claims and saying big things. It is a tacit assumption on everyone's part that everyone else has exaggerated and overstated everything, so some discounting would naturally happen in all conversations. Maybe it is just the culture of the place but sometimes the tall claims get tested. Once in a while the bluff is called.

Later that Christmas morning, Bouncy Boy (I learn that his real name is Jitendra), my two educated friends (Vinod and Shant) and I are sitting and eating a mid-morning breakfast of *jhal muri* (puffed rice spiced up with raw onion, green chilli, raw mustard oil and some *namkeen*). As usual, Bouncy Boy is making tall claims about all the nefarious stuff he will do once he gets out. Suddenly I hear a voice behind me.

'*Tu sooter banega?*' (Will you become a shooter?)

'Shooter' is locally pronounced 'sooter'. It means assassin. And the voice means business.

Jitendra gulps and looks around, panic visible in his eyes.

'*Kya, Bhaiya?*' (Sorry, Brother?)

'*Tu sooter banega?*' repeats a heavy-set man lying behind me.

Brief silence. Confusion and panic on Jitendra's face. Then he finally says, 'No, once I am out I think I will look for a regular job, Bhaiya.'

In a while the heavy-set man gets up and walks out. In hushed tones I am informed that he is a gang lord from a place called Wasseypur.

———

That day my name is called out (along with a bunch of others) twice on the PA system. We are all asked to report to the office—presumably to be assigned some work. On both occasions Ghani's guys tell me to stay put. So I do, but am apprehensive that some cop would walk in and ask why I did not come when called. Fortunately no one does.

Another announcement on the PA system calls me to the office along with all the other new entrants. This time I am instructed to go. We are to be photographed.

We all march to the inner gate and are let out into the corridor which I first entered last night from the other side. To my right is a door through which we are led. Inside is a large, bare room with a PC and a webcam. A guy is standing there with a digital camera as well. Like the others, I am handed a slate with my name and today's date, which we are to hold to our chest as we are photographed one at a time. I wonder if I should smile for the picture but decide against it. My slate reads 'Chetan Mahajan, 25/12/2012'.

Merry Christmas, Mr Mahajan—you now have jail-time to add to your résumé!

———————

In less than 24 hours I am a known name inside the jail. The newspaper coverage and the 'price tag' attached ensures I am on many people's radar. I realize that a two-crore embezzlement accusation makes me a juicy target for many. I receive a few veiled threats, and some not so veiled ones.

On my way back from the portrait shoot, I am accosted by three men. One of them is obviously the leader. The trouble-maker says that his kid-brother also goes to our centre, and so he also wants his money back. I do not say much but simply ignore and sidestep him. We are visible to the cops sitting in the courtyard so I doubt anyone would get physical here. After that I also plan to stay safely holed up in Ward 2.

The timing of my arrest is terrible. I am arrested on 24 December, just as the Indian judiciary goes on an eight-day-long winter break. The first bail process can only be started on 2 January when the courts reopen. And I am told by my fellow prisoners that the bail process itself will take a minimum of two days, which means I am here at least for 10 days if not more.

My company had appointed a local lawyer in a hurry, and he had come and met me on the 24th at the police station. He kept saying that courts would open on 26 and

27 December, but in the jail I find out that nothing will happen before 2 January. If my lawyer does not know when the courts will open, God only knows how long he would take to get me out!

Visiting hours in the jail are from 8.30 a.m. to 12 noon. I do not expect any visitors as it is too soon for anyone either from my family (in Delhi) or my company (in Chennai) to make it to Bokaro before noon. Predictably, nobody turns up till noon, and I settle to wait for the next day.

However, at 3.30 p.m. my name is announced and I am summoned to the entrance gate. All announcements are made on the PA system, which means everyone knows that when your name is called you would be at the gate soon. When I reach the thick iron-sheet gate I talk to the guard on the other side through a little face-sized window and tell him my name was just called. As the guard goes to check, I notice a guy waiting for me inside the gate. He casually strolls up to me and says

'*Bahar to bahut garmi kiye hain!*' (You've generated a lot of heat outside).

I do not respond.

'*Ab jail ke andar bhi garmi kar rahe hain?*' (And now so much heat inside the jail too?).

I give him a blank look, feigning ignorance.

'*Main samjha nahin,*' (I don't understand), I say.

'*Nahin samjhe?*' (Didn't understand?) he says. '*Koi bat nahin. Baad mein mil ke hum tuka sab samjha denge.*'

(Don't worry. I will meet you later and ensure you understand everything).

Just then, the guard unlocks the gate and I step inside. My father is waiting there. I am quite overwhelmed that he has reached so quickly. It is just so reassuring to see him! He looks tired and weary. I give him a big hug. I can see a tear at the corner of his eye.

Typically, a meeting with a visitor in the jail is across two layers of wire mesh placed three feet apart. You can only see the other person and talk. No touching or hugging or any such. Further, at any point of time you may have up to four to five different visitors meeting prisoners—so the noise level in the meeting area is crazy. Hearing anything is hard, and you have to shout above the din to be heard. Not a great way to have a conversation.

However, my father and I are allowed to meet in person in the privacy of a room—again because he is a retired army officer. He shares the update on the legal front. He has carried with him a desperately required change of clothes, a sweater, and a copy of *The Economist*, my favourite magazine. He also tells me that my brother is arriving the next day. I give him a list of things I need.

He tells me how the whole family and many friends had all huddled together till 2 a.m., and how he had left home at 5 a.m. to board the 7 o'clock flight. Then after the three hours in the cab from Ranchi to Bokaro and visits to the police station etc. he finally made it to the prison. The only reason he is allowed to meet me during non-visiting hours is because he is a retired colonel.

In his typical style my dad had met the jailer and superintendent on the basis of his own status as an ex-Army officer. He had then gone on to make a case for my innocence. While these senior jail officials could not free me, they had agreed to a certain set of concessions. The way we met—in a room like civilized people—was one. But the biggest change that my dad's visit brings about is that the jail authorities decide to move me to the hospital ward. They feel I would be more secure and comfortable there. So after our meeting, the 'Zamindar' (the most senior cop inside the prison) walks with me to Ward 2 and asks me to get all my stuff. Ghani and some of his cronies try to get a word in but finally choose to stay silent in the rather menacing presence of the Zamindar. I grab my few belongings, and follow the Zamindar to the hospital ward as the rest of the prisoners look on.

The Hospital Ward

The very first impression of the hospital ward is that it is colder and less friendly than Ward 2. There are 16 metal beds and 4 wooden cots in a room about the same size as Ward 2. There is a temple in one corner again at the other end from the loo. The people here just seem quieter and less lively, and there are fewer of them.

However, a bit of a circus starts soon after I enter. An old man (who everyone refers to as 'Budhva') is insistent on lighting a fire inside the ward. He has a *tasla* (round shallow metal tray) full of dried daatun twigs. He is trying really hard to light the fire, which for some reason refuses to catch. Everyone in the ward is generally kidding him, and making funny comments. A cop walks in presently, and advises the old man—as much as any Jharkhand cop advises a prisoner—that he should not light a fire inside the ward.

Given that the old man's cot itself is wooden, it is good advice. But everyone in the ward gets a good laugh out of it. The Zamindar talks to a boy named Raju—a dark, reedy youth who seems underweight and doesn't smile much. He seems to be the Vijay of the hospital ward.

Raju walks me to a metal bed and tells me that is where I would sleep. The once-white mattress is now a dirty-brown. I brush it with my hand to dust it and the cloud that appears is big enough to bring rain. Anyway, this is home for the next few days so I dust the mattress vigorously, spread my fleece blanket (which my father has just brought) on it, and try to get as comfortable as I can.

The cop comes by at 4.30 p.m. and shouts 'jora'. Everyone sits up in bed. The headcount is done: 15 + 2 = 17 (the two not present—Nageshwar and Aseem—are on duty). Even though nobody sits in pairs in the hospital, the headcount call of 'jora' stands.

The light in the ward is a CFL which is in the middle of the room—and close enough to my bed so I could just about read in its light after dark—and I now have something to read! The mattress—even though dirty—is soft enough for a decent night's sleep. A sight better than

Ward 2, for sure. The blankets are prettier but less warm than the ones in Ward 2.

The door had been shut at 4.30. I hadn't eaten dinner: it had been served when my father was visiting, and the Ward 2 people had promised to keep it for me. But now I am locked in the hospital ward.

A couple of hours later the two men counted in absentia at headcount—Aseem and Nageshwar—turn up. They make their introductions and ask if I have eaten. I say no, and they say that their dinner is kept aside every night. They share their dinner with me, and also tell me that I could pay a couple of guys in the ward who would be happy to help me with daily chores: collecting and serving food, doing dishes, washing clothes etc.

These two men are fixtures in the hospital ward: Nageshwar and Aseem. Nageshwar is the man who had met me along with the fish-face cop when I had entered the prison yesterday. Both Nageshwar and Aseem perform various official tasks (like Nageshwar was doing yesterday on my arrival) so they have some special privileges that other prisoners do not—including being able to sleep in a real bed in the hospital ward, being out after lock-up time and so on.

26 December 2012

My first night in the fabled hospital ward, I sleep badly. I am cold even in the fleece, mosquitoes keep buzzing and biting, and I toss and turn my way through the night.

In the morning as I sit in bed, I suddenly feel this looming presence next to my bed. I gently glance to my right to see a tall figure in a shiny-white starched lungi wrapped across a substantial waist. As I look further up, I see this body which is probably six-feet-one-inch tall, and at least 110 kg. At the top of this imposing physical presence is a teenage baby face just sprouting a beard and moustache. He says '*Pranam, Bhaiya*' and introduces himself as 'Gullu'. He says someone named Anuj Bhai wanted to see me. When I say I did not know Anuj, he says that Anuj is a cop from some local police station. The expectation seems to be that I ought to know of him. He adds that Anuj is asking about my well-being, and has called me as he wants to see me. I tell Gullu to tell Anuj Bhai that I am fine. I do not volunteer to reply that I would meet him.

Later that day Anuj Bhai comes and meets me himself.

A lean, tall young man, I would not have guessed he was an ex-cop. Certainly not what I expect in a '*bhai*'. He says that a certain Kishore Bajpai, who is the right-hand man of 'Vinod Khopdi' is asking about my well-being, and if I would come to Ward 9 to visit him. So I go along with Anuj Bhai to Ward 9, and am introduced to Kishore Bajpai. Both Anuj and Kishore are well-dressed, decent-looking young men. Kishore Bajpai is holding a cell phone very casually in his hand (cell phones are an absolute no-no in the jail). I am offered hot tea once I am seated. That is almost impossible in the jail, but in this ward they have a heater—which, again, is strictly against the rules. Kishore Bajpai says that the SHO who had arrested me had asked Vinod Khopdi to ensure my well-being inside the prison. He then dials a number and says that Vinod Khopdi wants to speak to me. I think this is the only time in my life that I have actually spoken to a 'Don'.

The conversation is brief. Mr Khopdi asks about my well-being. He repeats that the cop who had arrested me, SHO Surinder Singh, had called him and put in a good word for me. He adds that if I need anything—such as access to a cell phone—I should not hesitate to ask Kishore.

After that I speak on the cell phone to my wife and tell her that I am fine and safe. I also call my boss to talk about the work situation outside. It is a huge, huge relief to have access to the cell phone. After my calls are done some of the other residents of Ward 9 chat with me. They are all friendly and nice. However, they are all pretty convinced that there is no getting out of this jail quickly. They narrate stories of how they do not trust the legal system, and how despite strong, logical cases, their bail and release have been denied. I am polite, but reserve my opinion that my case is pretty different, and my alleged crime probably a lot less serious. Kishore also makes me an offer that I could move to Ward 9.

Ward 9 is easily the most 'posh' ward in the jail. In addition to cell phones, they have a heater, a TV with an iPod (so one could watch movies), bigger mattresses which are not shared, and only some 15-odd residents. They even have an inverter connection in the ward. The offer is tempting.

But I like the quiet of the hospital ward, and am not too sure about Ward 9, so I decide to stay put for now. But having seen these two other wards—Ward 9 and the hospital ward—it is apparent that Ghani and his crew had done a heavy sell job on me with Ward 2—taking advantage of my naïvety as a first-timer in jail. Ward 2 was an ordinary ward—just like any other. And in most respects it came nowhere close to even the hospital ward—leave alone Ward 9. Even if one wants to do drugs, it was available in practically any ward for a price.

Later that afternoon, my brother also comes and visits me. Both he and my father are doing everything possible to ensure my earliest possible release even though it isn't their job. They also are quite involved and engaged in the legal process. It is actually the company's job but nobody senior from the company has even visited me yet—on day three of my incarceration! It is disappointing to see that nobody senior from the company is based on the ground in Bokaro to take care of the legal matters. Only the local staff from my company has come to visit me.

With usual jail speed word had got around about my 'pairavi' (connections) inside the jail. Many prisoners know that I am allowed private, face-to-face meetings with my visitors. That the Zamindar has moved me to the hospital ward—on the instructions of the superintendent, no less—is public knowledge.

People start speaking to me more deferentially. None of the threats made earlier materialize. People are either pleasant or simply leave me alone. I know that my number one concern—safety—is taken care of.

Jailonomics

In jail all work is done by the prisoners themselves. They cook for themselves, clean the jail themselves. The librarian is a prisoner, as is the support staff in the office. All the farming inside the jail is done by the prisoners, and one can see brinjals, cabbage, cauliflower and tomatoes growing inside the prison.

I am sure that, to important visitors and in all their communication, the jail authorities paint a pretty picture of the jail—reminiscent of some kind of commune I would imagine in places like Auroville, or like a kibbutz in one of Leon Uris's novels. You would think the jail is one big happy family, living in brotherhood and harmony.

That's bullshit.

The fact is that there are two sets of people in a closed community, and only one set of people get to carry the *dandas*. All power and authority emanates from the stick, and the economics automatically is shaped and driven by this power and its complete misuse.

Theoretically, the jail is not supposed to have an economy at all. No cash is allowed inside. Shelter, food and very basic medical care is free for all prisoners. Prisoners are allowed to do some work, for which they are paid a tiny daily amount (22/32/46 rupees per day: the amount depends upon the nature of work) of which I am told a third is deducted automatically. The balance is deposited into a post office account somewhere, and can be tapped and accessed as required by the prisoner as long as he does not bring cash into the prison. But these amounts are a joke today, and well below what the government itself pays in schemes like NREGA, the National Rural Employment Guarantee Act.

The best way to understand the jail's economy is by looking at a couple of examples.

First, let us take the example of the imaginary Rajesh. Rajesh is from a middle-class family, and has been arrested because he is accused of some crime. I am making no assumptions about the nature of the crime or his guilt, which should anyway be irrelevant as he is an undertrial, that is, innocent until proven guilty (like everyone in this jail).

This is Rajesh's first time in jail and he has had no advice on what to bring, what to pack etc. The district police bring him into the prison and hand him over to the jail police (a different police force). Rajesh is scared and confused. Fish-face or some other on-duty cop is there to receive him. However, the police does not explain anything about money not being allowed etc. There is a yellow flex poster on the wall in the entrance corridor which spells out everything that is not allowed, but it is a long list, and reading it is not really something a freshly arrested man is likely to do. If Rajesh has any cash, what is to be done with it is his own judgement. Even assuming he has been informed about the option to deposit cash and other stuff at the entrance, many questions arise in his mind 'Should I deposit it? Will I ever get the deposited money/items back? Should I give some of it to the cops to have an easier time inside? Will I ever get it back? Can he help me with anything inside? Will I need cash inside? Will I be allowed to keep it? Should I try and hide it? If I try and hide it, and they find it on me, will I be beaten?

No answers. But unless he deposits the money at the gate, the fact is that any money he is carrying will be taken from him. Illegally.

Next, Rajesh is taken to a ward: in this jail, most likely Ward 2. From that instant on various inmates try to put a value on Rajesh.

Every new inmate in a ward is a potential source of income for the ward-in-charge. It is in the ward-in-charge's interest to keep Rajesh as scared and intimidated as possible. The fear of violence, mistreatment, torture and various other abuse is put into Rajesh—not just by the ward-in-charge but also by his various assistants and also other residents of the ward. After he is reasonably convinced he is offered a safe haven in Ward 2 itself—for a price. The amount I was told—and which I had agreed upon with Ghani is 10,000 rupees. Shant and Vinod told me (once I had left Ward 2 for the hospital ward) that they had paid only 5000 apiece, and the 10,000 they had mentioned was the total for both of them. If Rajesh finds Ward 2 too expensive or chooses not to commit, Ghani will ensure that the next day the cops will likely move him to another ward. The next morning, on the basis of the newspaper and conversations he has with various people, other ward-in-charges will make him offers. Simultaneously the jail cops will make him do manual labour and generally ensure he has a bad time to force a decision. Because Ghani will be upset with him for not agreeing to the deal offered, Ghani will probably ensure he has a terrible first day—he might be threatened by various people. Some minor thrashing—without any visible marks—behind closed doors is also very possible. In a sense it is like a very twisted auction system for a hotel website—but happening inside a prison.

Let us say Rajesh finally settles on Ward 2 on day one

itself. However, this is just an entrance fee. There are then ongoing costs of just being in prison—for example, to pay Ghani, Rajesh needs cash. Whatever cash Rajesh had is either deposited at the gate (if he is lucky) or taken by the cops. Currently he has no cash. Let's say Rajesh agreed upon 5000 rupees with Ghani.

Over the next day or two Rajesh has some visitors. He asks them to bring him, say, 10,000 rupees on the next visit. In the visiting area the visitors and the prisoners are separated by two layers of wire mesh with a 3 feet space between the two meshes. Plus there is often a cop hanging around—there is no way anyone can hand anything over and the visitors have to leave any items brought for a visitor with the cops before they can meet a prisoner. So the stuff (clothes/food) for Rajesh in which the money is kept is handed over to the police. The police search it thoroughly. They find the 10,000, of which they keep 2,000 and the balance 8000 is handed over to Rajesh.

Rajesh starts to settle in but finds the food terrible. In a place where the definition of tasty food is spicy and oily, the bland, boiled jail food is the farthest you can get from it. This is intentional. Only if the regular food is bad can Ghani (or any other kitchen-in-charge) charge a decent price for the 'premium' food he sells to the better-off prisoners.

Consequently, the regular food of the jail, for those who cannot afford the premium, is the worst possible in terms of taste or nutrition. Rajesh is then offered a price of

1,000 rupees per month for the premium food (which is better but only marginally, in my book). But after two or three days of regular jail food Rajesh finds the 'premium' food fantastic. Rajesh is also a smoker (true for a majority of the inmates), although not a heavy smoker, and now wants cigarettes as well. He understands that cigarettes are available, but at double the market price. Cigarettes are on the 'not okay' list, so the cops allow them in but charge a 100 per cent margin on them. Similar margins apply on ganja, alcohol, and even cell phones, but the more prohibited the item, the bigger the premium.

Rajesh is happy that cigarettes are at least available, and arranges for some. He also notices that he smokes a lot more in here than he did outside: partly because he is tense about his case, and partly because he has nothing else to do.

His family comes to visit him three times that week. On the third visit his family tells him that the cops charged 120 rupees for each visit after the first one. Rajesh is unhappy and tells them not to pay. He says he will take it up, but is not sure who to talk to. Outside each ward are tacked two bright yellow pieces of flex. One has the list of prohibited items: the expected stuff like alcohol, drugs etc. Plus, inexplicably, books (although nobody seems to stop them). The other flex is the daily and weekly dietary entitlement of each prisoner. Rajesh wonders about his rights as a prisoner but these are not clearly spelled out anywhere.

In week two his family doesn't visit him. When they finally meet and he asks about the delay, they say they came multiple times and waited to meet him but refused to pay. The cops told them to go away after a while. The cops told his family that his name had been called but Rajesh had not responded and was probably asleep. The fact is that his name had not been announced. Some inconvenience and wasted time finally teaches the family that to meet their beloved Rajesh more than once a week, a price needs to be paid. Not to the government, but to corrupt policemen.

After a while, Rajesh is looking for a break from the monotony of jail food, and wants to eat something from outside. Once or twice a week his family gets him home food, but obviously not what he wants when he wants it. In jail everything has a minimum wait cycle of three to four days. Since Rajesh has no way to communicate (Rajesh is not rich enough and nobody invited him to Ward 9—so he has no cell phone access), he can only tell his visitors in one visit what he wants in the next one. He learns that he can order food from outside, but again at twice the market price. Every once in a while the police conducts a *talaashi* (search) in his ward—and, if anything prohibited is found, he lands up having to pay even more.

Inside jail, Rajesh is not generating any income, or producing anything. Now to top it all he has gone from being a source of income to an expense for his family.

Let's take another example of Raju—again a fictitious character—a boy from a local village. He is from a poor family and has only studied till class 8. Again I make no assumptions about the nature of his crime or his guilt. The only thing to remember is that he is an undertrial.

Raju comes into the jail with few possessions. He had been advised not to carry cash. On his entry into Ward 2 he is carefully evaluated. The next day's paper would be important only if his crime is serious—otherwise petty crimes by poor people are often not considered newsworthy. The ward bosses try and assess him very quickly: is he a potential source of income? Is there potential profit in coercing/protecting/harassing Raju? If that does not seem the case then is Raju good as a worker to perform a variety of menial tasks? One of the ward bosses thinks Raju is a candidate for the 'worker' class. He can wash dishes/clothes/sweep and mop the floor, clean loos etc. They also try to assess whether Raju will do these things quietly and for practically little or no money—or will he make trouble?

Well, in Raju's case let us assume that there is no money that can be made off the boy. And Ward 2 has a good supply of workers so Raju is shunted off to another ward. His name is called for labour every day, and in his new ward they make him perform a variety of menial tasks. Raju believes he has no control over which ward he can be in, and also believes the ward boss has the authority and power not just to keep him but also physically beat him, he submits and falls into the role of the worker. Raju not only does not know his rights, he does not even know that he *has* rights! He is paid a pittance, if at all, eats standard jail food, and believes he has no rights or choices. His only hope is a quick implementation of justice for which he looks to his family (who are all illiterate) and his lawyer to get him out quickly.

When his family comes to visit, the routine is similar to Rajesh's except that since his family is visibly less affluent the cops are willing to let a visit happen for Rs 50 instead of Rs 120.

So there are two categories of people who take money from prisoners: The police, and a set of better connected and more powerful prisoners. I am calling them the 'uber-prisoners'.

Even uber-prisoners derive their power from the police. The police get to decide who will be the kitchen-in-charge: so they take a cut in all the profits from the kitchen. Similarly, the cop has the authority to decide who will be called for labour and who will not, and what the consequences are when someone whose name is called does not turn up. The cops get to assign prisoners to wards, and also move prisoners around. (My being assigned to the hospital ward is an exception because the jailer/ superintendent had taken the decision).

The power is with the cops, as is the greed. The cops pass their power along to ward-in-charges or other key players like Ghani, who use the power to squeeze profits out of the prisoners. Because their power is only 'loaned' to them, they are always effectively under the control of the cops. The cops always take a major proportion of the profits away, and the 'appointees' always try and save some extra profit for themselves. The reason why Ghani tells me not to tell anyone that the amount we have agreed upon is 10K is that he does not want the cops to find out. He will probably tell the cops 5K, and pay them accordingly. Interestingly, 5K is what he charged Vinod and Shant, but had me priced at 10K because he thought he could. In a sense I was being cheated, and would probably have felt wronged and angry if I did not have my analytical hat on, or maybe if the amount involved had been more substantial. And if I had actually paid it.

Every single one of these powers is used to make money. For example, a couple of days after I had moved to the hospital ward, Ghani met me. He said that to get me off the labour list he had paid some cops some money. (You would remember that my name was called in the labour announcement but I was told not to go, and nobody came looking for me). So I paid him the amount he asked me for—350 rupees. The point is that while the uber-prisoner (in this case, Ghani) collects the money, the power still flows from the cops and so a significant portion of the money also flows back to the cops.

The top cop inside the jail—and one of the most imposing characters in the jail is the 'Zamindar' (literally, that means land-owner). I don't know why he is given that title, but that is how he is referred to even in announcements on the PA system, so I guess that is his formal designation.

One look at the Zamindar tells you that he is the Zamindar. A tall, bulky man with a big stick and a bigger swagger, he wears two stripes on his sleeve, and a suspiciously jet-black moustache on his face.

Every morning he lines up all the new prisoners brought in the previous day and asks them who they are and what their profession is and what they are accused of. It isn't particularly pleasant, and many of the questions are meant to put the prisoners down. It is KYC, Zamindar style.

While I assume there is a legal reason to conduct this exercise, it certainly had other goals as far as the Zamindar is concerned. Firstly, it establishes very clearly in every prisoner's mind who the boss is. Secondly, it helps the Zamindar assess the potential worth of each prisoner, and therefore his ability to profit from him. The jail's whole economy is shaped by the power that flows from him.

Another thing that the cops lavishly dig into are the supplies provided for the prisoners. All the best food is appropriated and consumed by the cops. Whether it is namkeen, chiwda, chicken, or eggs, all these are made and offered first to the cops, and next to the paying prisoners. Tea for the cops is made multiple times a day with lots of milk and sugar. What the ordinary prisoners get is goat-piss.

The Zamindar sits comfortably in the sun every morning

and gets himself a shave from the prison barber. The prisoners—especially those who do not tip the barber—land up getting shaved with a used blade. In one case a poor prisoner who prized his long hair asked the barber to give him a slight trim—and got a crew-cut instead.

A few of the real mafia types are the only other prisoners treated with deference in the prison. The serious mafia inspire fear—not just amongst the prisoners but also the cops. The police feel that if they take too firm a line with that crowd, there could be repercussions. And people like me are treated with a little deference because we have the ability to reveal the entire system in great detail to the jailer and superintendent. Rumour has it that they are also in the know, and get a cut on everything. I have no way of knowing.

27 December 2012

With the arrival of my father and brother, all my material needs are taken care of: toothbrush and paste, towel, blanket and precious writing and reading material. And the one critical thing that I have longed for and missed inside the jail: running shoes!

Exercise does not seem too important to the average Indian, and prisoners are no different. Just like the outside world, few people consciously exercise, and even those who do are largely content with walking. My wife and I are both avid runners, and have run a few half and full marathons. We are both currently in the midst of training for a full marathon in Mumbai on 20 January. When I was arrested I was in formal leather shoes, and have been in these ever since. So it is a relief to swap them for running shoes.

As soon as I get my running shoes, I am itching to run. I expect to be out well before 20 January so do not want to compromise the training for the marathon. And more than the race, the training will also give me something on which to focus my energy while in prison.

The problem is that there isn't much space in the prison, and in the little space there is I would stick out like a pea on a bald man's head. So I don my running shoes on waking up today and step out with idea that I would do stationary running—just stay in one place and jog. Within 3-4 minutes of trying that I know it isn't going to work. In front of the hospital ward—inside the ward's boundary walls—is a very small space—so I just run loops there. While there is more space outside, I am still a little intimidated by the idea of running outside the ward compound. So I just run loops within the hospital ward compound. Each loop is 20 seconds. I run for 50 minutes. The repeated turns and slow speed make the run rather frustrating, but it's a start.

The sun god reigns supreme in a prisoner's life. That is because the ward door—made of really thick metal bars with a massive iron latch—is opened as soon as the sun comes up, and locked at dusk. In wintertime that means 6.30 a.m. to 4.30 p.m.: ten hours when one can be outside and move around, and 14 hours of being locked up in a room every day.

Breakfast, lunch, dinner and two cups of tea are all served within the ten hours when not locked-up. Breakfast is at about 8 a.m., lunch at 11.30 a.m., and dinner at 3.45 p.m.

The food is uniformly bad. Breakfast is either puffed

rice (murmure) with pieces of raw onion, or flattened rice (chiwda) with gur. On a really good day you might get sprouted kala chana (black gram). Lunch is rice with sabzi and dal. Dinner is roti with sabzi and dal. The dal is *always* the same yellow dal for both lunch and dinner—a thin watery soup where all solid matter settles to the bottom if you let it stand for five minutes. The sabzi is always potato, mixed with cabbage or cauliflower, or maybe beans. The only difference between lunch and dinner is that in lunch you get rice while for dinner it is roti. The rest of the food is largely similar and equally uninspiring.

In one sense it is health food as the food is mostly boiled and salted food with barely any oil, spice or flavour. According to the menu tacked outside each ward each prisoner is supposed to get either 100 grams of mutton (for non-vegetarians) or kheer—or Indian rice pudding—made from 500 ml of milk (for vegetarians) once every week. But that remains largely on paper.

The bandis (prisoners) try their best to improvise. Yesterday the prisoners from our ward had lit a fire in a tasla (metal bowl) with firewood managed from within the prison. They had also collected some brinjals and green tomatoes, which are grown within the prison, and roasted them. Once the skin is fully burnt from the outside, the vegetables were peeled, mashed and spiced up with some green chillies and salt. This 'chokha' is then served along with lunch. But given the number of prisoners it is effectively one spoon of the semi-cooked stuff apiece.

One of my biggest fears is that I will fall ill. I can handle life here as long as I stay fit, but I don't want to imagine being sick while in here. And for a mineral-water-drinking, street-food-avoiding city-dweller like me the risk is real.

All food is handled—and often served—with bare hands. Even when I saw the 'chokha' made within the ward, the vegetables were just mashed with bare hands in a bowl and not cooked again. Flies are all over. Dishes and hands are often washed just with water, without any soap.

I am given a steel glass and a plate as my utensils. The steel glass has a layer of black stuff stuck to the bottom. I scrub the glass clean with soap and mud till it has only steel visible inside. I also arrange for a spoon (nobody uses spoons here, I had to ask my brother to get one). I also try to stay away from stuff like raw, cut onions etc.

But I also think my system stays healthy because the prospect of going to the loo more than once a day is such an unwelcome one. In fact I am surprised I do not get constipated.

The water is the one thing I feel grateful for. The whole jail is fed by handpump water, which is much better than having to drink water coming out of a tank somewhere. I can pump it fresh whenever I want—at least when we are not locked in—and knowing it is groundwater, I am relatively comfortable drinking it. Even then, I have asked my father to bring bottled water when possible.

Beyond cleanliness, of course, also comes the nutrition aspect. Quantity is usually not a problem and I eat quite little compared to the average prisoner. I find the food very heavy on carbohydrates, but lacking in vitamins and proteins. There is the 'prescribed daily and weekly diet' which is posted outside each and every ward, but the actual food served is always short of that—especially in all the good stuff like meat or sweets. While I am able to supplement my diet with fruit, eggs and meat from outside, I feel that the regular inmate just does not get a balanced diet.

But I guess it is a case of classic 'talk-down' thinking on the prison authorities part: 'You get food, don't you?'

———

Both my wife and I love the outdoors. We are used to spending nights in sleeping bags inside tents while out on long hikes. Surviving on Maggi for a couple of days is just fine with me. I could reduce my physical needs for comfort to a basic level and be quite content with that. In here I have access to food three times a day, a bathroom, clean running water, and a comfortable if not cosy bed.

In a sense the jail reminded me of an NCC camp I had attended when I was in college. The food was basic, cleanliness levels just about okay. We slept on the floor in tents. The key differences, of course, were the mood, the company, and also the duration. And most importantly, the reason you were there.

At one level an NCC camp is like an extended picnic. Sure there is some hard work involved, but you are with friends and always working towards something. And each resident of the camp chose to be there. There is a certain positive energy in the very regimental set-up, and I think it largely came from the joy of youth and from striving for something bigger.

In the jail there is a certain pointlessness of existence. This is a jail for undertrials. Everyone in the jail is accused of criminal acts. Of course the nature of the crimes ranges from petty offences to murder. Bouncy Boy is accused of having stolen a cell phone. Vinod and Shant were accused of embezzlement (same section as me: 420). Kishore Bajpai, Nageshwar and Aseem are all in for murder of different kinds.

Everyone is just waiting. In limbo. The prisoners often have little control over the legal process being run for their release from outside, so they just wait for some word. It is a perpetual state of vacant, undefined waiting, locked behind 20-foot high walls on all sides which are impossible to scale. And once the basics of safety and comfort are taken care of, the biggest problem is boredom.

Cell phones are not allowed inside. TVs are in a select few wards, but not in the hospital ward. Even where TVs are there, you only get Doordarshan. There are practically no people in the jail with whom I have truly been able to connect. Sure I know people. We talk. I am always curious about everyone's stories as the whole experience is new and an education for me. But while I am friendly with everyone, I don't really have a friend.

To top it all we are locked-up from 4.30 p.m. onward.

The most difficult time is between 4.30 p.m. and about 9.30 p.m., which is the earliest I am able to sleep. The only thing I can do is read, except that the power supply fails way too often. So when there is no power one can just lie in bed and wait. Most people in the ward do just that even when there is power. They don't read. A few may talk. But a lot of people just lie in bed and wait.

Boredom very rapidly is becoming issue number one. I was curious about the library, of course, and had visited it yesterday. There is precious little in English—only two novels by Chetan Bhagat. I have never read him so I borrow *One Night at the Call Centre*, which I finish the same day. Not my usual read. And I thought the end was suspiciously inspired by *Life of Pi*. Had little desire to read the other novel by him after that.

It was on the very first day in here that I got the idea of writing down my experiences in jail. But I had no paper. It took me two days to arrange for some notebooks and pens, but since then this writing process has proved to be a great way to fight boredom. Of course it takes work writing pages upon pages by hand all over again—it's been decades since I last gave an exam which I wrote by hand, and everything one writes today is on the computer. But even rediscovering the feeling of pen on paper is fun.

I guess what also matters is one's personality type. I am not the kind of person who can just sit idle and do nothing. When I see people sunbathing by a pool or on a beach, I just don't get it. So for me to just hang around and do nothing is just very hard.

'I only wanted something else to do
but hang around'

Lyrics of 'Suburbia' by Pet Shop Boys

Thanks to frequent visits from my father and brother, I have some very useful things in jail: specific books of my choice, a booklight with spare batteries, magazines etc. Between reading, writing and some running, I am hoping that I will keep myself at least reasonably occupied during the day, and the running will also help me sleep better at night.

A critical device is the booklight—and has quickly become the mainstay of my existence in jail. The small booklight is battery powered, and it essentially means that the power failures do not prevent me from reading or writing at any time, even at night.

I am not sure how long I will be able to maintain this solitary lifestyle, but two weeks (which is more than the projected duration of my stay here according to the lawyers hired by my company) I can probably manage. I have an avid interest in World War II, and many of the books I have asked people to bring are about that Great War. Reading about Rommel's campaigns in Africa, or Churchill's six-volume history of the war can just transport me out of jail to a completely different place. Ironically, these are books I have owned for years but have never found the time to read.

The most versatile piece of cloth I have ever seen is the 'gamchha'. It is the true multi-tasking, all-in-one accessory for the Jharkhand man.

A simple rectangular piece of cotton cloth, typically with some sort of check pattern, it starts life as a towel: I dry myself with it after I have had my bath. However, since it is not made of towel cloth, it dries in a jiffy, and then gets into its act. Once dry, it quickly turns into a scarf or a cap. You will find people wearing it around their neck or covering their ears and head with it to keep warm. If you're enjoying the winter but the sun feels too bright it turns into a parasol. When breakfast comes around it becomes a plate—dry chiwda or murmure are easily collected in it along with gur or raw onions.

For khaini, cigarettes, matches etc. it turns into a pocket or a bag. After you blow your nose on the roadside it turns into a handkerchief to wipe your fingers. At night when the mosquitoes come after you it becomes a mosquito net with which to cover your face and still breathe easy.

When I got to jail, I asked my brother to get one for me instead of a towel, simply because a towel would stand out more. But as I have used it I have started liking it a lot. Besides, a towel would take forever just to dry out.

Of course, the lungi is as ubiquitous and as much a way of life as the gamchha. But it isn't even half as much of a hero as the gamchha. After all, a gamchha can always become a lungi. But a lungi substitute a gamchha? No way!

28 December 2012

With a better understanding of how the jail works, and more confident of the fact that people would likely leave me alone, I decide to venture out for a run today. The animosity many had expressed seems to have evaporated—or at least does not spring up around me anymore. I run loops again—of course. Inside a jail there is nowhere one can run to. But running outside the ward compound, and in the larger jail compound each loop goes from being a slow 20 seconds to one minute 10 seconds, which is certainly a whole lot better. Still not as big as I would like, but the fact that I am even able to run is something I feel grateful for.

Since I have no access to the internet or my training schedule, I decide to run entirely on instinct and follow what my body says. As per my marathon training schedule, I know I have to do one 20 km run around early January and then taper off for the full marathon on 20 January.

I feel pretty good today after my two runs from yesterday and today morning. I think I will do a longer distance tomorrow. Mentally decided on a distance of 16 km for tomorrow morning.

After the run I spend part of the day just wandering around the jail a bit. By talking to people I realize that there is a fair degree of variety amongst the various wards. Ward 2 is considered the 'Amad' ward (reception ward), and I have already described that earlier. Ward 9 didn't have a name but is clearly the most exclusive ward, both in terms of cost of living, and the company you get to keep. I guess it is the nearest to a five-star ward within the jail.

Then there is Ward 3 from which one can hear loud bhajan singing in the evening and also the conch being blown once or twice every day—the saffron ward. Another interesting ward is number 12. Evidently some kind of guru or yogi was a resident there for a few months, and he started teaching everyone in the ward yoga. He has since left, but the ward stayed with its yoga routine as a tradition, and this ward is called the yoga ward. I was told that yoga still happens there between 7.30 and 8.30 a.m. each morning. Always looking for an interesting way to kill time, I had gone and peeped in one morning, but instead of a class had found four or five men each doing his own thing. Since most had their eyes closed, and were deeply involved in their own meditation or activity, I quietly left.

Directly underneath it is Ward 10 a.k.a the Roja ward. The Roja ward is populated largely by the more traditional Muslim inmates. The 'God Wall' in that ward is adorned with a picture of Mecca instead of any Hindu gods or goddesses. Amongst the inmates one can see a few bearded and skull-cap-clad older men.

Then there is the ward which is dedicated to noble ideas and terrible implementation. I call it the 'Broken promises' or the 'Lost opportunity' ward. It is a ward in which nobody lives. But the ward is full of weaving equipment—not a little but a lot. And we are not just talking Gandhi charkhas, but much more complex (and expensive) equipment—worth tens of lakhs of rupees. When I tried to find out the story nobody seems very certain. Even Nageshwar—who has been in this jail for over seven years—does not remember a time when the things were actually used in any kind of productive manner, but the inmates said it is cleaned and dusted and shown off during all visits and official inspections etc. It is one of the government schemes on which so much money is spent, but which are doomed to failure because of the lack of actual implementation.

The 'Broken promises' ward stays locked and hardly anybody ever goes in or out. The equipment has collected a significant layer of dust. And 250-plus capable but directionless, idle men who could learn a new vocation and effectively produce something of value—and in the process feel worth something more themselves—kill their days hanging around making small talk and eating khaini all day.

The Old Man and Reiki

One of the residents of the hospital ward is a 62-year-old man named Virendra Singh, but most people called him

'Reiki Chacha'. He also claims (like me) that he has been framed for an economic crime for which he is not guilty. His version of the story goes like this.

Evidently Mr A had issued a draft in the name of Mr B, for which the acknowledgement had been signed by Virendra Singh, and in the acknowledgement he had clearly said that he is providing the acknowledgement on behalf of someone else. He himself is some sort of middleman and not even an employee—and had neither taken the money nor paid it. The payment draft was not made in his name either. But a case had been filed against him. It would've sounded far-fetched to me 10 days back, but now it sounded perfectly plausible.

Reiki Chacha has a head of thick, white hair and a moustache. Medium height and rather frail of build. Mostly smiling, he is good at making friends. He chats with all the people in the jail and is quite well-known. He knows some English and keeps insisting that the jail is a 'great university' full of 'cream persons'. He is always looking to bum a cigarette off anyone whom he meets. He describes himself as a 'Reiki Doctor' and he keeps talking about positive energy and the 'flow'. Often at strange times at night—2 a.m. or 4 a.m.—when I am unable to sleep and am tossing and turning in my bed or have to go to the toilet—I have noticed him sitting up all alone in his bed when the whole ward is asleep. His eyes are typically closed or half open, like he is in some kind of meditative state.

He has the knack of saying some strange things which are often out of context, and therefore quite funny. On one occasion there was a case being described by one of the prisoners about his friend who was in a relationship with a girl. After a few months the girl accused him of raping her. Reiki Chacha piped in '*Dheere dheere pyar ko badhaana hai, hadh se guzar jaana hai*' (Slowly we will increase our love, and then we have to cross the limit). This is a popular Hindi love song of the 90s—but rape is probably the last thing on the lyricist's mind!

When conversation turns to the difficulty of killing time in the prison, he invariably repeats the line '*Kaate nahin kat-te yeh din yeh raat*' (It hard to pass the hours of these days and nights): again lyrics from a Hindi love song, and again not written keeping a jail in mind.

Yesterday, three or four prisoners were hanging about enjoying the warm sun, Reiki Chacha amongst them. I noticed him looking intently at one of them. Very pointedly he said to him, 'You have some problem in the area between your shoulders.'

'Me? No,' replied the guy–who was probably in his late 30s.

'The flow is certainly being obstructed in that area.'

'Well, I was in an accident some one and a half years back, and had hurt my backbone then.' The conversation drifted on to other things, but I was a little intrigued. Agreed that the backbone isn't all between the shoulders, but a good part of it is. And this guy was a healthy-looking man. If it is a pure coincidence, it is an unlikely one.

So I decide to ask the old man to 'Reiki' me. There isn't a better way to describe it as I did not have a specific problem. I just want him to, well, look me over or 'scan' me and tell me what he saw. It is as much for entertainment as to satisfy my curiosity. He said he would 'Reiki' me provided I would pay his fees. And what is that? A packet of cigarettes.

I asked him which brand, he said '*Wills Flake pila deejiye. Woh bhi chalega.*' (Even Wills Flake will do). I later realize that Wills Flake is a really inexpensive brand of non-filtered cigarettes.

I request Aseem who is good at arranging for such stuff. He tells me that getting them is easy, but they would cost twice the market rate. I had told him to go ahead yesterday itself, but nothing happened. When I checked with Aseem last evening there were still no cigarettes.

Since I am keen to try out Reiki Chacha, I ask Aseem for the cigarettes again this morning, but this time I also gave him the money. That works better, and Aseem hands me two packs of cigarettes within a couple of hours. I had told him I only needed one, but he had misunderstood, so I had a spare pack as well.

I immediately give Reiki Chacha one pack. I am not a smoker but keep the other one aside. In the late morning most prisoners step out to enjoy the sun and the ward is relatively empty. I am lying in bed reading, and Reiki Chacha comes up to my bed and sits at the other end. He folds his legs, makes himself comfortable, and says, 'So let's get started then.'

I put my book aside. 'I don't really have a problem. Just want you to take a look,' I say.

'No worries. Let's just talk for a while and things will figure themselves out,' he says.

And so we talk for a while. He tells me how Reiki is actually a science and how he is only at level two and not level three so he could not teach it, and so on. In a while he said, 'The last three years have been difficult for you.'

I nod. Professionally and financially that is true. I had changed three jobs in the past three years as against two job changes in the 13 years before that.

'And you have some problem with your back—to the right side below the shoulder.'

That is absolutely wrong—there is no problem with my right upper back. I tell him the history of my injuries— left shoulder separation, broken right ankle, stress fracture. In fact, the one thing I had hoped he would pick up is a recurring spot of pain in my left shoulder which I had injured almost eight years ago. Even now when I exercise, a small spot of pain appears in the left shoulder—but that never appeared in his 'scan'.

Nothing had ever gone wrong with my right upper body. But he insists that I have a problem in my right upper back. And when I tell him about my left shoulder problem, he does not pay much heed. Says he cannot find anything wrong.

Then he asks, 'What god do you believe in?'

'No particular god,' I reply.

'Even then. Is it Shiv or Vishnu or some other?' he insists.

'No specific god. I am not religious.'

'Still there must be an image of some god in your temple.'

There is the implicit assumption that a temple exists in our house. But we did not have one. Both my wife and I are practically atheists—at least when it comes to organized religion. But I doubted he would be able to fathom that.

The nearest temple that I could consider 'mine' is probably the one in my parents' house. But I really cannot remember which god's images are in it. It has been a while.

'Laddu Gopal' he says suddenly.

'Huh?'

'There is an image in your temple of a baby Krishna with a laddu in his hand.'

I ho-hummed, still not sure. The image sounded familiar, but I guess it would be to anyone who has had even a remotely Hindu upbringing. I can just imagine a blue-coloured chubby Gopal holding a laddu in his hand.

Reiki Chacha goes on.

'You are three brothers right?'

'No, two brothers and a sister.' (But my sister is a well-placed professional who supports herself and her family. Maybe that makes her a son as per Hindu scripture?).

'Your brother has a problem with his right knee,' he said.

I know he has a problem with one knee. I am not sure which one. I tell Reiki Chacha him I am not sure which knee.

'Right knee,' he insists.

'And your sister has a stomach problem.'

My sister is gluten-intolerant—she cannot eat many normal foods like wheat or atta. So I guess that qualifies as well.

'Is your mother alive?'

'Yes.'

'She has trouble with her knees.'

That is bang-on. My mother has had trouble with her knees for some time now.

'Maybe it is a genetic problem? This knee thing?' he asks.

'Unlikely. My sister and I don't have it,' I say.

'You see, I cannot diagnose the problem for you. But I can tell you where the problem is.'

Well, I have to admit that so far he has got at least a fair number of things right. I am a complete non-believer in this stuff, and a sceptic at the best of times. But I had to ask some more. We had bought a new house three years ago—and I had changed my job also at the same time.

'Could this three-year phase have been brought about because of a new house?' I ask.

'I can see you have three houses'.

Not true. I had two. But then by a Hindu way of thinking my father's house is probably partly mine as well, I guess.

'Of the three, two are fine, but one has a slight problem. Your kitchen faces south?' It is part question, part statement.

I have to work this out in my head. I do not know offhand which direction my kitchen faces. And I also wonder what 'faces' means. Is it the way its door opens?

'The chulha (stove) faces south,' he clarifies. More statement and less question this time.

I think about it.

'Yes,' I say. I am a little surprised myself!

'You need to change that. You don't need to rearrange the entire kitchen. Just move the stove so it faces a different direction. Anything but south. No south-west or south-east, even.'

I start thinking about the logistics of that. We would have to install a new slab. The electric chimney would need to be moved as well. And where would the fridge go?

Nuts!

'What if I don't move it?'

'Then these problems will continue. South is the home of Yamaraj (god of death in Hinduism). And food is your fuel. You should change it.'

With Yamaraj entering the picture it is clear this is now getting into a dubious mix of Hinduism and Reiki. But the fact that he had got the southern orientation of the kitchen right still bothers me. There is only a 25 per cent probability of that.

The conversation moves to other things. He gives me

advice on meditation, which he keeps calling 'concentration' but I get the general idea.

Well, I don't know what I will do after I get out—will I actually rearrange the kitchen to reduce Yamaraj's influence on my diet? Most likely I will tempt fate. I rather loudly proclaim to people that mine is the most Vaastu non-compliant house in Gurgaon.

Buying into the mumbo-jumbo does not go with my self-image. Even though some of the stuff he said is pretty compelling, there were enough holes.

On the other hand, I really, badly do want this three-year phase to end—I mean, even right now I am an innocent man sitting in jail! But I really don't think moving my kitchen stove around will fix it. In fact, actually doing something like that goes too far into the irrational and superstition zone for me to buy into. If I did something like that then I would not be me.

29 December 2012

I wake up looking forward to my 16-km run today. Start at 6.30 with the gate opening, and run for an hour and 40 minutes. Time is a good approximation of the distance. I know my average speed is about 10 km/hour. I feel quite okay after the run, although my feet hurt a little.

But being out there and running for almost two hours is probably considered insane amongst not only the prisoners but also the cops. I do not realize how much till later in that day when this young man—a complete stranger, probably in his early 20s—walks up to me.

'*Pranam, Bhaiya*' (Greetings, Bhaiya).

'*Pranam.*'

'*Kya aap commando hain?*' (Are you a commando?)

I laugh out loud.

'No. Who said I was?'

'Outside they are all saying you are a commando.'

'Who is they?' I ask.

'You know, the prisoners and the cops and all . . .'

'No. Please tell them I am no such thing. I just like to run.'

He persists. 'How can you run so much?

'I just like to.'

'But still, it must be really difficult,' he says.

I think of the three rules of distance running I had coined:

1. Identify your fatigue threshold.
2. Ignore it.
3. Repeat step one.

Just as I start to open my mouth he says, 'And why run at all?'

I shut my mouth. The chasm is too wide and deep to fill. So I just say, 'It not that difficult if you build it up over time. Start small and increase how much you run slowly.'

He hangs around a bit longer and then leaves. I can tell that he simply does not get it. And I have no way of explaining.

———

After the first two to three days in jail I have a backache. Initially I cannot figure out why, but in a bit I realize it is because there are no chairs at all in the jail. We have the floor and the walls. In the ward we have metal hospital-style beds. We also have some improvised stools. But no seating with any kind of back support.

That is when I realize just how habituated I am to sitting in chairs with decent back support. It does not seem to bother anyone else. I guess it is the nature of my workplace. The absence of a table and chair is very irritating to me—especially since I want to write a lot.

A couple of days back I had noticed a full-size office desk and chair in the 'clinic'. Nageshwar, my ward-mate and the prison paramedic has the responsibility of—and the key to—the clinic. Nageshwar is basically a very decent sort. Quiet, stays focused on his work, of which he seems to have a lot. I ask him if I can use the table and chair when the clinic is open. He readily agrees and has mostly been quite a sport about it. In fact, yesterday he even left me in the clinic by myself as he went about his business elsewhere.

My writing and reading is now done much more comfortably at least three to four hours a day. And my back has stopped hurting.

The clinic is also a source of information and entertainment. The other day this guy turns up at the clinic holding a cloth to his upper lip and tells Nageshwar '*Blooding ho rahe hain*'. (Blooding is happening).

Turns out he cut his upper lip while shaving. Single-edge razors are the norm in small-town India, and certainly inside the jail. I looked at the cut—it seemed rather deep. I asked him, 'How did it get cut so deep?

He replied, 'Since I did not have a razor I just shaved holding the blade in my hand. There is always a rix in that.' 'Rix' is the standard pronunciation of the word risk in here. I have to make a conscious effort not to laugh about the rix of blooding. The guy is bleeding too heavily.

The language spoken here is also interesting, and even entertaining in its own way. There is, of course, the customary 'va' added behind all words. So bag becomes 'bagva' and book becomes 'bookva' and so on. All numbers are followed by 'go' so three becomes 'teen go' and so on.

Then there is the language which is more specific to the jail. Colloquially, the way to say someone is nuts is to say 'he has a screw loose'. In the jail that now has a new context altogether—anyone losing it described as '*Uska tower chod raha hai*', which means 'He is disconnected from the tower'. Initially I do not get it but then it is explained that the phrase alludes to a cell phone without a connection to a tower. And, of course, there is the rix of mispronouncing certain words.

In common speak no private body part or female relation is spared. The standard language spoken would be described as filthy in many circles. For example, Raju's favourite phrase is '*Dadi kochodo*' (Fuck your grandmother). Except he does not say it to anyone in particular. He says it all the time when he plays ludo: for example, if he wants a 3 but gets a 1. When he wants to actually abuse someone—like the pujari—he uses other abuses which are more commonplace.

But filthy is a strong word. It's not actually so bad—it grows on you after a while.

While there is a lot of bravado on display, there is virtually no conversation about sex. Sex is the one thing that truly seems taboo in the jail. There is probably a lot of quiet jerking off that goes on. Some pornographic magazines do the rounds in the jail—we're talking rather cheap Hindi porn here. The talaashis keep those also to a minimum.

On my arrest and during my first day or two I feared that the jail would be full of forced sex and physical violence. While there is some physical violence, the sex aspect seems very, very quiet. Like most of small-town India, there are many taboos to talking about sex. I thought maybe the men were shying away from talking about any such thing with me, but I have never even overheard any conversation involving sex here—and overhearing conversations is the easiest thing to do in jail.

Then there is jail humour which works only within the context of these walls.

'If Tulsidas was here today he would be in jail. The case would be a copyright act case because the original Ramayana was by Valmiki.'

Another one is about Hanuman wanting to meet Ram in heaven, and having to bribe his way through. He did not carry money, so gives away his crown, his mace and also his tail to various babus and gatekeepers along the way. Finally, the last official refuses to believe he is Hanuman because he has no mace, tail or crown, and shoos him off. Finally, he calls Lord Ram, and Ram tells him things would have been much simpler if he had carried some banknotes to pay the gatekeepers.

I sleep briefly today during the day. Unusual—maybe it is tiredness from the run. I dream that I am a German tank commander in full uniform leading a pack of Panzer tanks. It is strange though because I am roaming the streets of Bokaro in my tank leading the Panzer Unit, and I am in a Nazi uniform.

Today in the morning as I stand in the sun after breakfast, a rough-looking, bearded man walks up to me and hands me a photocopy of a handwritten report in English.

'Please read this and tell me what it says,' he says in Hindi.

I take the paper from his hand and glance through it. It is a post-mortem report. I read through it in detail and tell him, 'This is the post-mortem report of Baby Lata. It says she died of poisoning.'

I read further.

'It also says it is not clear if she committed suicide or if someone else gave her the poison.'

He thinks briefly. Then says, 'So it is not certain that the death is due to poisoning?'

'No, it says clearly that the child died of poisoning.' I just assume it is a child since the name started with Baby.

'The report is not of a child. It is of a woman. Her name is Baby.'

'Okay. It says clearly that she died of poisoning. It just says it is not clear if it was suicide or murder.'

'Okay,' he replies tersely. Takes the report from my hand and leaves.

Must be a Salman Khan fan. No sorry, no thank you.

I think about it later. Firstly, little babies don't commit suicide. Duh!

Secondly, the correct set of options for my response should have been, 'It is not clear if it is suicide or murder or accident.' Somehow the third option simply does not appear in post-mortem report. Or in my mind.

30 December 2012

As I feel more secure and comfortable in my new surroundings, I have also started talking to more people and learning more about the jail. There are many questions one can ask directly, but many that one cannot. I also realize that some people hesitate to speak openly in front of me because they feel that I will stand in judgement, and probably judge them harshly. Being in a jail myself I try my best not to sit in judgement.

This jail is a small one with 275-odd prisoners. This includes some eight to ten women in a separate building, who are completely isolated in their own section of the jail. The men have no interaction with them. Importantly, everyone in the jail is an undertrial, which means nobody here has been convicted yet. The only convicts here, I think, are Aseem and Nageshwar and they also both have their cases in appeal.

I obviously do not know all 275 inmates, but have had conversations with many, and would broadly classify the prisoners as follows:

This is a rough categorization. There are grey zones that

The Bad Boys of Bokaro Jail

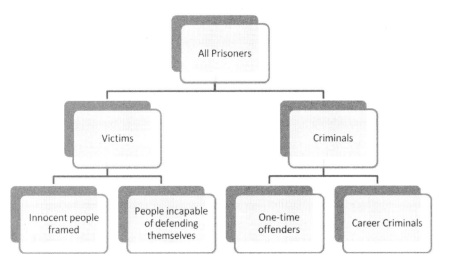

exist—for example, some of the innocent people framed are also possibly guilty. It is impossible for me to say. Similarly, many of the people incapable of defending themselves may actually be guilty. But in my view they are victims nonetheless.

Before I dig further into these categories, let me say that at one level everyone in here is a victim of the legal system. Only a select few know how to use it to their advantage, and those people rarely land up in jail.

Now let us take the first category: victims. These are the people have either been duped by the law and arrested, or people who have committed some petty crime, but have received a disproportionate punishment because they do not have the wherewithal to protect themselves.

Within victims the first category is innocents. Of course, I am no authority to say who is innocent or who is not. My examples are based largely upon what they claim, and also upon their behaviour and interaction.

A good example of an innocent is Akhilesh.

Akhilesh is a teacher from Bokaro. Says he teaches Biology to classes XI and XII. After saving up some money he had bought a used car. He lived with his parents, who already had their car. He had bought the car to ply it as a taxi and make some income from it. One day, the cops came calling and asked to see the papers. They told him the car in his house was a stolen car. He gave them all the details of the seller, but evidently the seller's employer bribed the cops with 3 lakh rupees and got him off the hook, and Akhilesh was arrested instead. He is in the hospital ward with me—I ask him why he is in the hospital ward. 'The cops beat me for five days to try and get me to confess. I was badly hurt.' As I talk to Akhilesh I sense a very deep anger and pain within him.

Now Akhilesh, who is deeply religious, spends six or seven hours every day praying in the corner of the room in the temple area. He says if he will not do that he will go mad just repeatedly thinking about what happened. Praying keeps him sane. Often when he is not praying he just lies in his bed, sometimes with his face covered.

Since he is now medically recovered, the order has come for him to move to a regular ward. He does not want to move because he is afraid that other wards will not be as peaceful and quiet and he would not be able to pray. So he has bribed the Zamindar to allow him to stay on in the hospital ward.

The second category is those people who are effectively unable to defend themselves, and are at the mercy of a highly flawed legal system. Education is the first factor in this. Many of the inmates are men with little or no education, thus making them completely dependent upon other people for legal recourse. The second factor is connections. Even if one is illiterate, if one's family is well connected (admittedly a rare combination), there could be some rescue possible.

This category also includes people fundamentally too poor to even afford bail.

These people are the most needy, yet the most exploited. Lawyers ask for any amount of money, give false promises, and are often complicit with the prosecution. Their goal is not justice for their client, but the maximization of their own income, even if it means an innocent person spending years in jail.

This category includes people like Jabra and Raju. Jabra is one of the residents of Ward 2. He is accused of some petty crime—bicycle theft or some such—and had been granted bail. However, he is in jail because he is unable to produce the 2500 rupees required: 1500 for the bail and 1000 for the lawyer's fee. He has been in jail for over four months already.

Raju is one of the boys in the hospital ward who, along

with Makar, is my paid help inside the prison. Raju is probably 18 years or thereabouts (he isn't sure). He is accused of rape and murder. Again, I have no way of knowing if he is guilty or not. I asked him about his case, and he knew the basic story. A girl had been raped and murdered in his 'basti'. He claims he was at home along with his parents and brother at the time. However, some people in the basti told the police they suspect him although they had not seen him commit the crime. On the basis of that he was arrested. He says that the medical report is clean—but when I ask exactly what that means he is a little fuzzy and quite confused. On one hand he says that he will probably be sentenced to prison as the only suspect. On the other hand he says that since the medical report is clean he should be released.

The next hearing of his case is in January, and he is hoping for the best. He has also filed for bail in the high court.

Raju has studied till class VII. His parents and brother are outside and are leading the legal battle. His parents are illiterate, and his brother has studied till class X. He says his brother has found him a good lawyer. I sincerely hope so!

The question here is not whether or not Raju is guilty, but that even guilty people are entitled to a decent defence. The circumstances of the crime need to be understood, and judgement passed accordingly.

There are quite a few other similar cases that fit into this category. These people are at the bottom of the proverbial pyramid, especially when it comes to being able to manage a legal defence.

The next category is the one-time criminals. I will cover this tomorrow. Tired.

———

One of the prisoners wears a T-shirt which says 'Only God can judge me'. Appropriate in a prison! I doubt he knows what it means so I ask him. He has no clue.

I wish it were true, though. Not just in the after-life, but in the jails of Jharkhand as well.

31 December 2012

No run today either. Resting and recovering. Morning chai and I have started writing.

The next category I have created is one-time criminals. These men are not criminals by profession. But have committed, or are accused of committing, a significant crime. The difference between the last category and this one is that these folks have the ability to understand and use the legal system for their own defence as well. In fact, I would say a big chunk of prisoners fall into this category.

Examples abound. The most common are the Dowry Act cases. In the case where the wife is dead (which seems to be the vast majority), guilt becomes hard for the accused to deny. Most of the men involved in this are young. Late twenties or early thirties. Statistically, it is highly unlikely that so many young women would die of natural or accidental causes in the single district of Bokaro. Whether it is suicide on the wife's part, or some form of murder on the husband and his family's part, the prime accused is the husband. The thinking and mindsets on issues like dowry are often driven not by an individual, but by an entire family. But if any one person has the ability to alter the thinking and bring about change, it is the husband. Besides, it is he who swears to protect and take care of his wife. So I think it is only fair that he is considered the prime accused.

Both Aseem and Nageshwar fall into this category: both their wives have died within a few years of marriage. So does Anuj, the ex-cop who is a resident of Ward 9. Another example of this category of one-time criminals— although not a dowry death case—is that of a lawyer, Ashok Choudhary, who is in charge of Ward 1. Evidently he suspected his wife of having an affair with another man. The lawyer was afraid for his own life, as he felt that his wife and her lover had conspired to kill him. Or maybe he was just plain angry. The story goes that the wife's brother was also fully aware of the situation, and felt his sister was in the wrong. So the wife's brother egged on the lawyer to kill her. Eventually, the lawyer shot and killed his wife (or stabbed—there are two versions going around. I have not asked him which one is true, and don't intend to).

After committing the crime, he is said to have walked into the police station along with the murder weapon, and confessed. Made front page news for four straight days, I am told.

Another case is that of Pappu Ansari. He is accused of murder in a property dispute. His version is that he got into an argument with someone he had sold some land to.

The buyer had encroached on additional land. The argument got intense and the buyer of the land brought out his rifle. However, the buyer himself, by mistake, shot his own son dead and injured another of his own henchman. The only defence the buyer had for himself was to accuse Pappu and his family of the murder.

After the incident the buyer had the police file an FIR not just against Pappu but also many of his relatives. Consequently Pappu, his two brothers, his father and also his father's two brothers are all in this jail: his clan alone makes up 2 per cent of the jail's population.

But, as is obvious from the profiles, none of these were career criminals. Most men in dowry cases have led regular lives as citizens. Pappu Ansari is a property dealer. Ashok Choudhary is a lawyer.

My last category is the one comprising career criminals. There were some people like this in the prison, but few that were truly dangerous. Many were simply petty thieves. Kishore Bajpai and other people like him would top this list on the 'dangerous' factor. In all my conversations he has been very friendly and respectful. He said he is himself highly qualified—says he holds an MCA degree. Evidently, at one time he ran a big and successful business which employed over 70 people in Noida. He is from a family of highly qualified people. But he himself says that he has a 'streak' because of which he got involved in some illegal dealings. He has built a career in crime, and is currently accused of murder. He told me that he was arrested two days after the date of the murder he is accused of. Unlike most others, he never claims innocence.

When talking about crime and jail he also says, matter-of-factly, how ganja is a good distraction, and how he is now addicted.

Another story is of a Gujarati man in Ward 6, whom I have not met. I again, have no way of knowing the true story, but from what I have heard so far I have put him in this category. The case against him is one of flesh trade: evidently he was trying to buy a girl. His version is that he came to Jharkhand to get married because there is a shortage of marriageable girls in Gujarat, and consequently, the men there are coming to Jharkhand to get married. Fine so far, except he was paying the family whose daughter he was marrying. Evidently, someone else present at the ceremony also asked for 1500 rupees. When the 'groom' refused, the miffed relative called the police.

While I can accept the basic premise of the story (shortage of girls in Gujarat), a man paying to marry a girl in a place like Jharkhand, where grooms are traditionally given exorbitant dowries, is a little too hard for me to swallow. Hopefully, the courts will establish the facts.

Actually as I think about this category, Ghani Bhai also fits squarely into it. Legend has it that he does everything possible to get into jail, and stay here. Stories abound as to how he will steal something or the other from a police station, and then keep it visibly on display as he eats in a dhaba or hangs around someplace close by, hoping to get arrested. Or how he will himself call the cops to report a theft, and then will start trying to break a lock as soon as he sees them arrive.

They say he likes it in here. He makes good money—the general guess is that he earns 20 to 25 thousand rupees every month that he is inside the jail. In here he has an assured supply of ganja, and a lifestyle he likes. They say he thinks of the jail as his office.

So I guess Ghani is also a career criminal as well, but for a completely different set of reasons!

1 January 2013

Slept early last night and through the midnight hour. Not that I have anyone here to hug or kiss or celebrate the New Year with. But I start the year on a positive note with a one-hour run. Have enough energy to throw in a sprint in the last couple of loops.

The PA system announces that the jail authorities wish all the prisoners a Happy New Year. A pair of massive speakers are brought in and music is played all day practically until lock-up time. Most of the music is rustic rural disco of some sort. One particular song is interesting: the lyrics went like this:

Hum toh hain Cappuccino
Tum pee lo zara haseeno

(I am like Cappuccino
Drink me up beautiful woman)

Dinner that evening is *kheer-puri*, an unusual treat. Party-time, jail-style.

My resident support group outside the jail has also seen a partial change. My father had arrived in Bokaro on the

25th evening itself, and my brother had reached on 26 December. While my father has stayed here all through, my brother left on the 29th, and my brother-in-law, also a good friend, come to Bokaro on the 30th, and has spent New Year's Eve at a shady Bokaro hotel. My entire family seems to have postponed New Year celebrations till my release.

My heart really goes out to my father. He is seventy-three years old, and long retired from the army. He knows me as a very upright, honest and clean kind of person (similar to him in many ways), so it is very hard for him to fathom how I could be in jail. Further, the way things are done in the legal process in a state like Jharkhand is filthy and blatantly corrupt, and very hard for him to deal with. The fact that the company has also been slow and unclear about how to move forward—the fact that they still don't have a senior, responsible person on the ground in Bokaro to fight my case—is something that really troubles him.

The challenge of how to kill time is mounting. The default mode is to keep thinking about when I will get out of here. The court is—finally—supposed to reopen tomorrow. I am told the company has made all possible preparations to get me out within the shortest time possible. But this seems to have been largely arranged over the phone, and through my family members as proxies for the company. They know fully well that I am innocent, and have all the possible proof and resources to ensure my release in the least time possible. There is an appointment letter which states clearly that I joined only on 3 October. I am only an employee and not an owner or a board member—those are the people typically liable in any such offence. These facts should be enough for them to make a powerful case for my release.

I would have thought that bail could be obtained in two or three days, but Mr Ajay Shetty, the legal person representing the company told me that I should plan for 7 or 8 January, as it might take that long. He had visited Bokaro for two days and left after appointing a lawyer. I keep telling myself—and people who come to visit me— that I am mentally reconciled to being out only by 10 January. But the fact is I would like to get out tomorrow.

Evidently, three other colleagues from my company— including a legal person and an HR person—visited Bokaro from the head office last week. Amazingly, all three have gone back now, and none of them felt it necessary to come and meet me!

Anyway, to get out of this fixation of thinking about my release, and to make the most of my 10 hours of relative freedom, I try and make caricatures of people in my head. But I am a lousy artist, so the caricatures have to be verbal.

Another interesting resident of the hospital ward is Mahto-da. Mahto is a very common last name in these parts, and Da is just a sign of respect (literally meaning elder brother), which is automatically attached to his name given that, at age 50 or thereabouts, he is much older than most prisoners. Unlike people like me, Mahto-da is one of the deserving residents of the hospital ward. He has a serious medical condition because of which he is unable to walk normally. He is able to walk only on absolutely flat surfaces, and that too very slowly. He cannot sit up, get out of bed, or sit down independently. Even on slopes, stairs etc. he needs to be supported and sometimes physically lifted. On my asking, he tells me that he had contracted polio 10 years ago. I am surprised as I thought polio only happened to kids, but he told me that is not so.

Mahto-da is a loud, authoritative man but affectionate in his own way. He is a kind of honorary uncle to the various young men both in our ward as well as the juvenile ward. Whenever he needs help to get in or out of bed, or climb up or down stairs, or sit on the floor for a meal, one of the boys is around to physically pick him up and move him.

The rumour is that he is a member of the Ilyas gang. Ilyas is supposed to be the don of the coal mafia of Bokaro. But Mahto-da never brings it up, and I do not ask. Evidently, Bokaro, being an industrial town focused on steel production, has a mafia for various commodities such as coal, iron etc.

Within a day of my moving to the hospital ward, he talked to me at length about his son—a student at a polytechnic who, after he completes his three-year diploma next year, wants to convert it into a BTech degree by studying another three years. I asked Mahto-da more about his son. Evidently the kid is academically strong, and Mahto-da's pride in him is evident. The boy had cleared an entrance exam to get into the polytechnic, and had also won a scholarship. The polytechnic is a government institution so the fee is quite low. But if he chooses to move on to do his BTech, the cost would be substantial, and Mahto-da would need to take a loan. The ability to repay the loan would depend upon the salary his son would earn after his BTech.

I tell him broadly how to evaluate engineering colleges, which types to avoid, and how to determine the placement/career options realistically (as against the sales pitch every college would make). I also emphasize the importance of English and how the boy should make efforts to improve his English—especially spoken—as that could be a huge and often ignored factor for placement.

He hears me out and gets the gist of what I am saying. But after that, the next three or four times we speak his only question to me is, 'Job *lag jaye ga na, sir?*' (He will get a job, won't he, sir?)

Mahto-da is desperately seeking a guarantee for his son's future. He is just a father wanting the best for his son—just like my father camping outside. I wish I had some way of giving him such a guarantee—but I do not. And when I think about some of the engineering colleges I have seen, it makes me shudder.

The education business is seen as a major investment

opportunity by many moneyed people with the goal of multiplying their wealth. Per se that is not entirely bad, but most such people have little or no understanding of how to build and run a good academic institution. Consequently, much capital has flowed into the education industry over the last seven to eight years, much of this into engineering and management education. Medical education is another area where demand is potentially massive, but the growth there has been less rampant because of much more restrictive regulation which limits scale.

Engineering and management colleges, however, have seen a mushrooming of new institutions, most of which have appeared over the last seven to eight years. And this unfettered growth has resulted in a massive oversupply in the marketplace. Take the example of a town like, say, Yamunanagar in Haryana—10 years ago there were only two engineering colleges in the district. Now there are nine. The capacity of the district to produce engineers has gone up from approximately 600 to over 3000 in 10 years. The district population, in the meanwhile, has growth at approximately 20 per cent, as against the seats having grown at 400 per cent. Now, such disproportionate growth is not bad for the economy as long as there is job growth to support the increased supply of engineers. The economy (read 'jobs') itself has grown some 125 per cent . So where do the remaining 1500-plus engineers who graduate every year go? And this is the picture of just one district.

So against two colleges, each with an annual capacity of

300 each, you now have nine colleges with a capacity of, on average, 300 each. Except that this average number is highly misleading. The older, better established colleges continue to attract the better students and fill up their seats, while the new colleges have empty classrooms. So to attract more new students each college makes completely overstated promises in terms of placement and salaries. The intake levels are regularly compromised. And the students that, five years ago would never have made it into engineering courses are now given admission. These kids are allowed—in fact encouraged—to dream well beyond their realities. These dreams—the promises made by unethical institutions to gullible parents like Mahto-da— are believed by the parents. Many such parents land up taking loans for such an education, but after the degree the 'engineer'—assuming he gets a job at all—makes nothing close to what is required to pay the loan back. To make it worse, such loans in India are always made to parents and never to the student, and may often be made against collateral.

The sudden increase in enrolments has come about by severe dilution of intake standards. This also means that most students granted admission are unable to cope with the academic requirements of the programme, which are typically set by a governing university. A direct consequence of this is very low pass rates amongst students of the newer colleges.

The rampant growth of private for-profit education in

the absence of effective regulation is costing too many people too much. The irony is that these institutions are all 'non-profits', and fail because of their inability to make a profit! Personally, I am glad that many of these are shutting down.

So, despite my warning and guidance, chances are that someone like Mahto-da, and also the cop who frisked me on my first night, will be sold an unrealistic dream for their kids. Mahto-da will then take out a big bank loan for his son's education. The engineer son will graduate, and then discover that he is barely employable, and makes barely enough to pay for himself, leave alone his father's bank loan.

Of course, I hope Mahto-da's son is truly bright and makes it into a good engineering college which guarantees his future, but it is impossible to evaluate that on the basis of what Mahto-da has told me. He does not know how much his son scored in the milestone exams, or what kind of salaries the graduates from the polytechnic where his son currently studies make. I can only cross my fingers and hope for the best for him.

One other person I am getting to know—and like—is my walking partner, Pappu Ansari. Pappu is probably 30 years old, and has a moustache on his rather fleshy face. He has a quiet, ready smile, and is otherwise taciturn by Jharkhand standards. He is of medium height and build, and has a small beer belly—except it cannot be that because he doesn't drink. He loves food though, and the belly belies his fitness level, which I know because we have often walked together for two hours or more. His teeth are stained yellow with nicotine, although I don't see him smoking too much. Maybe he eats a lot of paan.

While he is someone I am very comfortable with, in terms of backgrounds we could not be further apart. He comes from a very well-known family of Bokaro—the Ansari family. It is actually interesting to hear him describe it. He says that the family resides in a single, large block of buildings as big as the open space in the jail—which is huge. Evidently, it is a squarish piece of land with a big courtyard in the middle, and buildings on all four sides. The size of the Ansari family is 400 people—some four or five generations seem to co-exist, and all uncles, aunts and kids share the same space. He makes it sound like a very cohesive, organized system. For example, he says that the family 'committee' has appointed specific individuals to handle all the legal aspects. He and his six family members all get their food from the extended family—it is delivered daily to the prison. The family of 400 does not have a single common kitchen, but rather it is 40 separate units living together. That means 40 kitchens in the family. They take turns sending food to the jail so it is not any one family bearing the burden. Similarly, the job of delivering the food is assigned to two young men from the family who make the trip six days a week (no visitors are allowed on Sundays).

In our many walks together initially, we have a lot of conversations. During our conversations he explains many things to me—society and how things work in Bokaro, the property market there (he is in the real estate business), the relevance of the different festivals in the Muslim faith and so on. He also asks me about my life and faith and God etc. I told him I am not religious. His response is simple.

'*Insaniyat se bada kauno dharm nahin hai.*' (There is no bigger religion than humanity).

As time goes by our conversations become less busy. After a while it comes to a point where we simply walk together without saying anything for as long as 10–15 minutes. But it is a comfortable silence.

Another reason I like Pappu Bhai is that he is more interested in the actions of people than in what is professed or what rituals are followed. I talk to him about his own marriage—which is unlikely to happen as planned because of his arrest. He says that he will only get married once the case is closed. I think that is fair. He also says he wants to have his nikah (wedding) in the winter, and his reason is the most interesting. He says weddings in their family are on a huge scale, and a vast amount of food is cooked. A lot of it is not consumed, and invariably spoils in the summer. However, in the winter months it does not spoil and can be distributed amongst the poor the next morning. A real, rational, practical reason to plan the timing of your wedding. That resonates with me.

Then, of course there are Nageshwar and Aseem. On most nights Nageshwar, Aseem and I have our dinner together. At lunchtime I often end up eating alone as Nageshwar and Aseem are busy with their other duties, and eat their lunch very late. Other prisoners typically eat lunch when it is served, which is too early for me. But at dinnertime it is nice to have at least one meal which is slightly more social rather than sitting alone and eating.

So each night around 8 p.m. Raju digs out a mat made of sack-cloth and spreads it out on the floor, and three plates are laid out. There is only one serving spoon so that is used by the three of us to serve whatever is on offer. Any goodies or special treats anyone has—say from a visitor—are shared by all, and also with Raju who also eats at the same time. Till then it is a really pleasant experience.

But by the end of the meal as both Nageshwar and Aseem start their burping and belching routines, I feel like I am caught between two erupting volcanoes.

2 January 2013

Today I see the whole system play itself out before my eyes.

I wake up early and am in my running gear at 6.30 a.m. waiting for the gate to be unlocked. Finally the cop comes, but unusually, does not call out 'jora'. The ward door is unlocked briefly, Aseem is let out, and the rest of us are locked back in for another hour. Evidently 'talaashi' (search) is being conducted in some wards, and when that happens, all other wards are kept locked. I have to satisfy myself with some stretching and strength exercises, and decide to postpone the run to the next day.

My ward mates seem to know the drill. Evidently these talaashis happen quite frequently. Today it is Ward numbers 2 and 3 which are being searched.

'So will the tea and breakfast also be late today?' I ask Nageshwar.

'No. That is why they let Aseem out. He will give the milk for the tea in the kitchen. And they will also let two to three other prisoners who cook go to the kitchen,' comes the response.

That day a lot changes on the food front. Ghani, who is the kitchen-in-charge, loses control of the kitchen. The story floating around had many versions but I could gather the gist of it. Ghani used to charge certain prisoners (including me) for special food—like the small cup of better tea that followed the regular jail 'goat piss'. The cops were supposed to get a cut, which he had not been paying enough of. However, evidently, a fair amount of cash was found on him, and that didn't go down well with the Zamindar.

Various other things are found in the talaashi. Some chillums and ganja, some alcohol. A cell phone is also found in Ward 3, hidden inside a box of agarbattis.

Later that day as I sit writing in the clinic, Jabra from Ward 2 turns up. He had a red welt on his left forearm. One of the cops had hit him with his lathi during the talaashi. As Nageshwar cleans the area and puts some ointment, the stinging causes Jabra to break into such a string of abuses, he could have won a declamation competition.

Coinciding with the talaashi, for some reason Ward 9 suddenly comes under massive scrutiny, and my access to cell phones virtually vanishes.

The day goes in gossip about the outcome of the talaashi. Many prisoners hope that better food will now follow. Dharmendar is made the new kitchen-in-charge. With Ghani's exit, today the regular dinner is much better than usual. Let's see how long that lasts!

The evening lockdown happens as usual at 4.30. A couple of hours later, the door is unlocked, and a new prisoner is let in. A short, bearded man with a big belly and a bandage on his left wrist walks in. He looks really sad and troubled. Raju tells him which bed to sleep in, and then the usual questioning commences.

He is not entirely coherent, and weeps once or twice in between. After piecing everything together what emerges is heart-breaking.

The man's name is Umesh. He is a manual labourer at the steel plant. He had been married but his mother had killed his wife (he doesn't say why, but everyone automatically assumes the reason is dowry). He has since remarried, and now it seems his mother is on the verge of killing the second wife as well. To protest he tried to kill himself by slashing his own wrist. (The bandage on his wrist is the reason he landed up in the hospital ward.) However, that didn't work and he is still alive. He then decided to take a more certain path, and decided to jump into one of the blast furnaces inside the steel plant. However, the gate-pass on which he tried to enter the steel plant premises was a forgery and he was caught. The guards at the plant questioned and eventually arrested him, and so he landed up in jail.

Talk about a great start to the New Year.

3 January 2013

I catch up on yesterday's run today: run an hour, and am feeling pretty good. Am thinking maybe I will do the 20-km run tomorrow.

I go to Ward 9 hoping to make a call to my wife today. The phone has no balance left and I am told to wait a while, but just then my name is called over the PA system. I have visitors. I go to the office and meet my father and brother-in-law. I ask if I can call using their phones, but while they are allowed to meet me in person, their cell phones are taken from them before they can meet me. So no calls are possible then. After the visit I head straight back to Ward 9.

Two cops are standing at the gate to the Ward 9 compound. They are loudly rebuking a couple of prisoners. I just keep my head down and walk past them into the building compound. One of the cops calls out to me.

'You!' His tone is harsh.

'Who, me?' I turn.

'You're not from this ward, are you? Don't go to other wards. Go back to your own ward.'

'Okay.'
I turn and leave.

One of the things that you cannot help but notice here in prison is the number of young people. I am 42 (and I think I look it) and in here I am often referred to as Chacha or even 'Uncle'. The average age of the jail resident is definitely below 30. Even on my first night as Ghani Bhai and Bouncy Boy Jitendra sat eating their dinner, I had asked Jitendra, 'How old are you?'

'20', he had replied.

I had thought of asking 'Years or months?' But had decided against it.

'Really? 20 years old?' I had asked instead.

'That's what they put down on paper. I think I am around 16 or 17 years,' he said sheepishly. In rural India, for people to not know their exact age or their birthdays is not uncommon.

Ghani had smiled and said '*Bachha hai*,' (He's a kid).

I have heard people refer to me and also other English-speaking, senior management types as the 'CNN-IBN crowd'. I actually don't watch CNN-IBN, and my favourite news channel is BBC, but you get the idea. The implication is that we get a very different version of the truth. That we are informed, but disconnected from the realities of the real India. The experience of being in jail moves me very quickly away from the 'CNN-IBN' to the 'Doordarshan' crowd.

Every TV channel these days mentions and refers to the 'demographic dividend'. This phrase is meant to describe a bulge in the youth population. India right now has a disproportionately large number of young people—especially when compared to the developed countries. Interestingly, even China does not have such a large youth population—a direct outcome of their one-child policy. However, this youth bulge is not unique to India—the same phenomena exists in the Middle East, and in Bangladesh and a whole variety of other countries.

This demographic dividend is usually talked about in the context of how it represents a huge opportunity for India. Many people sound very gung-ho about this dividend, talking about how India will supply the entire world's labour shortages single-handedly. Well, so will Bangladesh, and Egypt, and a host of other countries. These eternal optimists seem to assume that Europe and the US will welcome schoolteachers, nurses, plumbers, electricians and other quasi-manual professionals with work visas and fat salaries. When I look at the 'prove-me-wrong' data or 'disconfirming evidence' (a phrase they taught us in B-school), it is a scary picture. What is often ignored or talked about only in much quieter tones is the massive curse this boon can quickly turn into if not harnessed and channelled into productive efforts quickly.

Crime rising drastically. Ghettoed enclaves of rich people with armed guards like one reads about in Brazil and many parts of Africa. Can't ignore that alternative possibility.

As I look around me at my fellow prisoners inside this jail—like Jitendra—I realize that I am actually in the middle of this youth population bulge. And from what I can see, most of these youths are busy twiddling their thumbs.

India has 500-odd districts, and each has on average one or two such jails. Let us put the number of jails at 700. Nageshwar tells me that there is a monthly intake of about 45–50 people, so we can assume that there is an annual flow of 500 prisoners in each jail, of which half are in the 15–30 age range. That is 500 x 250 = 1, 75,000 youth annually. Even if the assumptions are on the higher side, and the actual number is lower, that is a number of around one million youth between now and 2020—the year that the government and policy is taking as the target date for making this youth bulge employable. And this, not counting the jails where the convicts are sent.

The average population of the jail is about 275—but for simplicity's sake let us assume 250. That means each prisoner in the jail is incarcerated on average for six months. When you look at the duration of the average 'vocational training' programme in the market or conducted by the government, that is a positively long time. These young men are literally a captive population with no shortage or time. Only intent needs to be found.

Of course, it is easily argued that the boys and men who really need access to alternative employment skills are the ones inside the prison. Unfortunately, the jail exposes them to the exact opposite of a positive, constructive environment. Instead of having access to learning and growth, they become victims of greed and corruption.

4 January 2013

I am out of the gate the moment it opens and run a full two hours (approximately 20 km) today. My longest run till date inside the prison. That is 103 loops in two hours. How I wish the damn loop was longer than 70 seconds!

Running offers a great time to think and also talk. Typically, when Vandita and I run together, we run at an easy pace so that we can keep a conversation going. And even when I run alone I rarely use headphones or an iPod.

Running is a great time to let one's mind drift and just let thoughts evolve and tumble around in one's head. It is very meditative that way. As I do my run inside the jail I think about the reason for corruption, and come up with an equation for corruption:

$$\text{Corruption} = \frac{\text{Greed x Power}}{\text{Systemic Control}}$$

Greed is a starting point, of course. In a situation where there is no greed—say, in the case of a truly honest bureaucrat—the lack of greed will mean a zero there.

The second factor to which corruption is directly

proportional is power. If you have a lot of power, your potential to be corrupt is massive. If you have no power, there is nothing you can misuse. The obvious reason for the musical chairs that is 'Indian Politics'.

The third factor—which is the most effective way to limit corruption—is what I am calling systemic control. By systemic control I do not mean an individual factor like principled behaviour. Principled behaviour goes under greed.

By systemic control I mean the strength of the various laws and institutions to limit and control corruption. When Anna Hazare starts a revolution to create 'Lok Pals' and give them strong sweeping powers. That is really an effort to enhance the systemic control. But the reason why the Lokpal Bill has eventually stalled in getting through the Indian legislature is because it requires the ones with greed and power to apply systemic control. It's like asking hyenas to pass a law banning non-vegetarians.

And you can see what starts from the top reaches all the way to the bottom in the Bokaro Jail.

Today the superintendent comes to the ward along with another senior police officer in uniform, and a couple of guards. It is a ward inspection. He generally makes a lot of noise—asks why trash has been thrown outside, and that it should be cleaned and soon. He then specifically asks Akhilesh, 'Why are you in the hospital ward?' Akhilesh tells him he has chest pain and a BP problem. The superintendent asks him what medicine he takes for his BP problem. Akhilesh fumbles. He cannot come up with a name.

The superintendent specifically picks on him, saying that he prays too much and that the jail is not a temple. He also asks Akhilesh why he eats so little. Evidently, Akhilesh eats very sparingly. Later on when I ask him why—his stated reason is that he can sit in meditation longer, and he can focus on his prayer and meditation more when he is not too full. It is pretty obvious that the superintendent has been fed information, and someone has reported the 'odd' behaviour—too much praying, too little food. So the authorities are picking on him just because he is different.

Akhilesh, on his part, seems really afraid of any change. I had seen people pray for at least two to three hours in Ward 2. And I would imagine that a ward like the 'saffron' ward or the yoga ward would be okay places to pray and meditate. But Akhilesh has never been anywhere else in the prison. He has stayed in his shell, and never interacted with people outside the hospital ward. In fact, now that I think about it I have rarely, if ever, even seen him outside the hospital ward.

I guess in such a state it is easy to develop a fear of the unknown—in this case, other wards.

I also met Jabra again today. Got chatting about why he is here.

'What case are you in for?'

'*Maar peet ka case hai.*' (Got into a fight)

'I heard your bail is granted,' I say.

'Yes, but someone outside needs to pay Rs 1500 to the lawyer and Rs 1000 for the bail. I don't have anyone outside willing to do that.'

He is pretty matter-of-fact about it. I am amazed—2500 rupees between a man and his freedom.

'So how long have you been here?' I ask.

'I first came here as a juvenile in 2002—in that ward,' he says, pointing to the juvenile ward.

'In what case?' I ask.

'Same case,' he says. So the legal proceedings have been on for over 10 years.

'How long have you been here now?' I repeat my question.

'Five months,' comes the answer.

However, as I talk to other people I am told that the '*maar peet ka case*' is actually registered as a case under section 307—that is, attempted murder. How grave his crime actually is, I have no idea. But the small bail amount indicates it probably isn't that serious.

———

Really want to call home today, but in the morning I see Kishore Bajpai leaving the jail for a court appearance. Normally, those prisoners going to court return only after sundown—and lock-down—so no calls today either.

5 January 2013

Today is rest from running so I open up my notebook at first light and start writing. I realize that the more I write the more questions I have, instead of answers.

———

My case was supposed to have been presented at the lower court for bail yesterday. I am guessing it was turned down—that is what was expected by the lawyer. After that rejection, the lawyers expected to proceed to the district court today and file the bail application there today. Keeping my fingers crossed.

Lots of action in the ward today in the morning. Late last night for some time there was a cat somewhere, repeatedly mewing away. Woke me and a few other people up, but since she was outside and we were locked in we could not do much.

In the morning, a tiny kitten walks into the ward. Nobody wants it in the ward as everyone keeps food and stuff around and it would be at risk. And for some reason people just don't seem to like cats so much. I would have loved to keep the little guy—kittens can be so much fun! Anyway, it took four grown men 10 minutes to chase the poor little thing out of the ward.

———

Later in the morning, I go across to Ward 9 to try my luck at speaking on the phone with my wife again. I choose a good time. Kishore has just woken up and is having his morning tea. However, the reception I get from him is visibly colder this time. I am not asked to sit next to him (although he is alone)—he stays where he is and motions for me to sit on a makeshift stool across from him. Tea is duly brought around and I take the proffered cup, but as I wait he doesn't smile, and ignores me for a bit, reading the newspaper.

In a while one of the guys in the ward hands him a cell phone. He turns it on, and calls someone. He speaks briefly, and it sounds like he is speaking to his mother. When his call is done, I ask directly

'Can I make a call today?'

'You want to make a call? Okay.'

But even though his call is done he does not offer the phone to me—instead, he puts it in his pocket. There is another person in the ward also speaking on a cell phone. I guess maybe he wants me to use that phone, so I sit there waiting. He does not clarify anything, and somewhere I realize that he wants me to ask for the phone—wants me to acknowledge verbally that he has privileges and power in this jail that I need.

Kishore isn't making much effort at conversation. In a bit, I speak.

'So does this talaashi impact you as well?'

'Absolutely. It makes our life difficult.'

'Well, in the hospital ward things stay relatively quiet,' I say.

'I don't know why you continue to stay in that lousy place with all those diseased people,' Kishore says. 'The doctor can ask you to leave any time he feels like it. You know this is a much better place for someone like you. I know it is more money, but you're in prison now—you have to be here as long as you have to be here—might as well make the most of it. Basically, it is like choosing a better hotel—and facilities like a cell phone cost money: I spend 50,000 rupees just on that!'

Clearly, he had a cost that he needs to spread across more people. I think seriously—if I get out next week because of a district court ruling, then it makes no sense to move now. But if things get dragged out then having access to a phone would be a huge plus. But I am hopeful that the release will happen within three to four days.

Well, I have to say that Ward 9 is much brighter and airier than the hospital ward. You get half-decent, hot tea whenever you want it. There is a TV. The place is cleaner. Dinner is served hot because of the hotplate in here.

My problem is that these guys are nocturnes. They sleep at 2 a.m. and wake up at 11 a.m. And I am a morning person. But an even bigger factor is that I would be living in the company of career criminals, and would also strongly and visibly be linked-up to one. A part of me is very wary of that.

Anyway, right now I just want to talk to my wife.

'Kishore Bhai, my case is in court and I will find out by next week how things are going. A release might happen soon.'

'Don't expect a rational legal process here,' he warns. 'This is Jharkhand.'

Not only Kishore but all other people in his ward always paint a pretty dismal picture when it comes to the possibility of my bail. It is in their interest to make me believe that nothing will happen fast.

'I know,' I reply, 'but as you know my case is a little different. I am just an employee of the company accused in this matter.'

He shrugs, 'Let's see . . .' His voice is full of doubt. Does not sound hopeful at all.

'If a release is imminent next week then it makes no sense to move,' I tell him. 'But if it goes into the HC and stretches longer than I will probably move to this ward,' I lie. It seems to satisfy him for now. The guy on the other phone finishes his call.

'Can I make my call now?'

He nods, and tells the other guy to hand me the phone. After five days I am able to speak to Vandita.

I desperately hope the release happens next week!

Pappu Ansari is one of the few people with whom I am starting to form a rather tentative friendship. He is accused of murder, but I don't judge him on that. He is a straightforward and unpretentious man, whose basic philosophy of life I agree with. I often walk with him and that is how I am getting to know him. As we are out walking today, I tell him about the Ward 9 phone call bit. Don't share that with too many people—it is a little risky—but I think I can trust him. However, he has been round a lot longer than me in the jail, and tells me another story, which is a good reason for me to stay away from Ward 9. This story involves a south Indian prisoner whom I have never met, but have only heard of. He is no longer in this prison. Let's call him Mr Iyer.

Mr Iyer was also in for some economic crime. Evidently he was well off, and when he landed in jail, Ward 9 was an automatic choice. Now there is a regular mafia activity consisting of threatening well-off people with dire consequences, and collecting protection money on the basis of that threat. Very similar to the *hafta* in Mumbai. It is called *rangdari* in Jharkhand. The honourable tradition of rangdari does not recognize the boundaries of jails, and so, very often, calls for rangdari would go out from inside the jail. Since the walls are porous, and people can easily smuggle phones in by paying the right people, these phones could also be used for making rangdari calls. Mostly, the people who get these calls stay quiet and pay up, in which case it does not matter where the call has gone from. But every once in a while, someone reports a rangdari call to the cops, and then a big commotion would happen in the media. And, of course, for the media it is particularly juicy when the call has gone out from inside the prison!

When such a rangdari call is reported, the police would work doubly hard to trace the call. The person who received the call obviously can give the number from which the call has been received. And with cell phones it is possible to trace which location the call has gone from. The cops' standard operating procedure then is to track down all other calls that have ever gone out from the same number, and try and triangulate back to figure out who made the call in the first place.

Once, tracing one such rangdari call, the police landed up at a lady's house. Her number had been called frequently from the number used to make the rangdari call. They asked her if she knew anyone inside the Bokaro Chas Jail, and asked her whose number this was, and his relation to her. Cornered and with little option, she revealed that she was Mr Iyer's girlfriend. Now, Mr Iyer was a respectable, married man. But obviously in addition to a regular family he also had a girlfriend on the side.

The Bokaro police could smell an opportunity—not just to close the case but also to make money. So they blackmailed Mr Iyer into getting a fat payoff otherwise they said they would let the secret out. Evidently, that was the end of the relationship between Mr Iyer and his lady-love, and having lent his cell phone to people in Ward 9 also cost Mr Iyer a couple of lakhs.

Now, I don't have a girlfriend, but when I hear this story I realize that if I make a call to my family from one of the Ward 9 phones, and the same phone is used for a rangdari call, the police can just as easily reach my home and family as well. That's a chance I certainly do not want to take.

Finished reading *The Rommel Papers* today. Heart-breaking in the end. A classic true story of a brilliant general—but who was fighting for the wrong side. The book actually had me sympathizing with the German army and the foot-soldiers (not the concentration camp aspect: Rommel had nothing to do with that). In the end Rommel lost in Africa not because of any shortage of effort or bravery or skill, but because of something much more mundane—supplies. Food, equipment, ammo. He lost because of a shortage of the working capital required by an army.

I flatter myself by trying to draw parallels between his situation and mine (at work). It is increasingly obvious that I am fighting for the wrong side as well.

6 January 2013

It is a cold morning that starts with another talaashi. I have tossed and turned a good part of the night, and really do not feel like getting out of bed early or running, although I had planned to when I went to bed. Instead, I decide to go for a walk and do some freehand exercise later in the day as an excuse to stay in bed now.

It stays grey all day. The sun does not come out at all. The prisoners light a fire as early as 4 o'clock that evening.

———

The doctor came for a visit today. There isn't a fixed time or date for his visit. No predefined schedule. He seems to visit largely when he feels like it. The word spreads quickly when he visits, and a line forms of the prisoners who want to see him. And that is what they get to do—literally. They just see him. He sits back in his chair with his hands behind his head, and asks the prisoner:

'What's the problem?'

The prisoner typically gives a short description of what is wrong. On the basis of the description, the doctor tells

Nageshwar what medicine is to be given. And that's that. He never touches a patient. Never picks up his stethoscope, or looks into anyone's eyes, ears or throat. He sees about 30 patients in 30 minutes. I guess it's called hands-free medicine.

The doctor also cross-questions the residents of the hospital ward, and a few people are 'discharged' and moved out to the regular wards. Evidently, Nageshwar told him that the superintendent had asked that I should be in the hospital ward, and the doctor is okay with that for now. Hopefully I will be gone by his next visit.

The doctor's visit makes me think about prevention versus cure. And fundamental to that is the level of hygiene maintained in the prison.

The general level of cleanliness outside the actual room of each ward is approximately the same as a badly maintained railway platform. It starts with the toilets, which are exactly what you would expect in below-average highway dhabas. The one toilet inside the ward is supposed to be used only during the period of lock-up and again is usually quite filthy. I had made it a practice to pee the last thing before lock-up, and then pee first thing in the morning to ensure I don't have to use that loo.

Both outside and inside, all the water needs to be pumped and carried to the toilet as there are no flushes or taps. The toilets are so dirty and smelly that all the prisoners prefer to pee outside them. Consequently, a section of the compound wall also becomes an open urinal, and the smell prevails outside the toilets as well. Some 10 yards from this open urinal is one of the two handpumps. This one is where everyone bathes and washes clothes etc. The other one is used largely for washing dishes. Both have open drainage which forms a large sludgy pool of filthy water at one end of the ward compound. This is just one compound—now you can multiply that in scale five to six times for the entire jail.

I write another rather desperate letter to Vandita, which I hope I can deliver in person.

I also finish reading *The Difficulty of Being Good* by Gurcharan Das. Excellent read but takes some time and patience to digest.

At 4.30 p.m. they announce my name on the list of people required to go to the court tomorrow. Not sure if this is for a hearing or simply for attendance, and nobody seems sure. I am told one is handcuffed and then has to walk around in a public place so am certainly not looking forward to that aspect of it. But I have heard some other prisoners talk about how they were able to get in front of the judge, and make a case for themselves in person. I am hoping I will have a shot at doing that tomorrow.

I just want to go home!

7 January 2013

Am up well before 5 a.m.—toss and turn in bed for two hours. I am excited about presenting myself before the judge and being able to plead my case in person. 'Sir, I am just an employee, and have joined this company less than three months back. I have never collected any money, or taken any money in my name. I am not an owner, or shareholder, and am not on the board. Moreover, my employer is more than happy to co-operate. While all this happens can I please be released from prison? I have already been in jail for 15 days.' I have gone over the lines a hundred times in my head: I hope he will be convinced.

The ward door is unlocked at 6 a.m. and the call for 'jora' happens as usual. I go out and run for an hour to let off some steam. I finish the run and then shave, bathe and get into my best 'formal' outfit—blazer and all.

The other prisoners describe the court visit as quite an ordeal. It is my first time so I have no clue what to expect. I keep a book. Just to be on the safe side I check with my fellow prisoners if that is okay, and they unanimously say that taking a book is not just an okay, but a very good, idea. They also say that it can take all day and one cannot eat anything, so I should eat substantially before I go. So, at 10 a.m., I have a big meal and then after our names are called out for assembling in the office, I go into the corridor and wait.

I am the first one there and in a while all the men called turn up. There are twenty of us. A dark-blue police truck backs into one set of gates, and the outer gates are then shut behind it. The inner gate is opened after that. Our names are called out and one by one we all board the truck. The entrance to the truck is from the rear, and the truck has thick wire mesh windows, and a wooden bench along each side. It also has two sets of doors and locks at the rear, with a small space between the two doors for the cops to sit. The twenty of us go into the main hold of the truck and sit down, and the inner door of the truck is shut and locked. Then two armed cops get inside the smaller section and sit there on guard, and the truck sets off.

Bokaro is entirely unfamiliar to me but I recognize the court as one of the places I had visited on the day of my arrest. The truck backs into a police compound across the road from the court. We are all carted out and led into a large, stinking cell with stone benches. A row of toilets in the middle is the perfumery.

I read my book (the first of Winston Churchill's six-volume Second World War history) to keep my mind off my surroundings and the smell. After two hours my name is called. I am then taken from the cell along with another prisoner—we are handcuffed together, and the handcuffs are tied with a rope which is held by a cop. In this manner we are paraded across the busy road between the police station and the court. We are first taken to a courtroom, where the other prisoner's lawyer is waiting for him. He has a chat with his lawyer, and is asked to sign a paper. I had been told of the court visit date—so usually the lawyers also know and are there to meet you. I could see that people were waiting for the other prisoner—his lawyer, and some family members were there to meet him. However, no faces are familiar. None of my lawyers or colleagues. After he is done I am led to another room. There a clerk opens a register and I am asked to sign. I also sign and we are both deposited back in the stinking cell. No judge, no hearing and no chance to appeal anything.

It is very disappointing not to have made my case or seen a judge. I could mope but it will really serve little purpose. I try to read some more but I am not really able to focus consistently. So I get up and stretch and walk around. The walls are full of heart-shapes which have been dug into the concrete. There are numerous 'I love you' messages along with names of people scribbled all over the walls as well. It got me thinking of the time I had proposed to my wife—on 11 February 1994. That is the first time we had said 'I love you' to each other. It was a huge deal back then. Still is. Even now we repeat it to each other very often—when I am not in jail, anyway. After I proposed and she accepted, we were apart (in different cities) for 18

months and we had both struggled to be together. I had
changed my job to be in Mumbai which is where she was,
but she had to leave soon after I got there. Finally, in June
of 1995, she had been accepted into the Master's
programme at the Tata Institute of Social Sciences (TISS)
and we were able to be together. And we have not been
apart for more than three weeks ever since. I hope Bokaro
doesn't change that.

As I think about all this I also realize that we have
known each other for exactly 26 years—we had met on
6 January 1987. And we have been completely in love
with each other for 19 years. Over the years our love for
each other has actually grown.

Thinking of all this makes me smile. Makes me feel a
little better. Suddenly 15 days extending to 20 does not
seem like such an ordeal as long as I know I have true love
to go back home to. Just thinking of this gets me through
today. But also makes me miss her.

We finally get back to the prison at 6 p.m. I had just
spent eight hours to sign one piece of paper. I am put back
in the ward (after being very thoroughly searched) and it
is dark. There is no power. At that moment—and for the
first time since I reached this blasted prison—I really want
a drink. But there isn't one to be had. I remember I have
some cigarettes (the extra pack I had got with Reiki
Chacha's). I dig them out and light one. Reiki Chacha—
always looking for a freebie—immediately jumps across
and asks for one. I oblige. He lights up and immediately

parks himself on the bed next to mine and starts his usual mindless chatter. Rather bluntly, I tell him that I am in no mood to talk. He leaves me alone.

Smoking is alien to me—I have never been a smoker. This particular cigarette does give a brief buzz but I finally abandon the cigarette halfway. I can feel the nicotine aftertaste in my mouth for hours afterwards. I hate it.

───

While waiting at the courthouse cell, a lot of new prisoners are brought in. These are people who have surrendered before the court that day: mostly young guys against whom cases have been filed for petty crimes.

One of these new prisoners is an old man, visibly a traditional Muslim. White kurta-pyjama, skull cap. White, flowing beard. He is bespectacled, and crying. The cop who brings him in tries to comfort him with a few kind words, as do a few prisoners.

I ask him what case he is in for. He says 'Harijan' ka case. Intrigued, I probe further. He says that the accusing party has claimed that he and his family are practising untouchability, and not allowing them to use a public water source—some tap or pond of some sort, from what I can tell. His description isn't too clear and still punctuated by sobs. Evidently, he has been accused once before, but that was one or two individuals who had accused him and he was able to get out of it, but this time 10 people have signed an affidavit, and so here he is in prison. The old main claims complete innocence for himself and his family. I am extremely conflicted after talking to him. Strong developing nations with histories of inequality need laws that enforce equality. I wish I could be more confident that these laws were not being misused. For this old man's sake.

8 January 2013

After yesterday I really am not so up and about. I feel low and disappointed. But I do not want to succumb so I force myself out of bed for a run. I stop at twenty-nine minutes because I am just seething with rage, and my thoughts are going round in a closed loop. I cannot believe the way Everonn/Gems is handling this entire legal process, and is leaving so much to chance. They still do not have a full-time person based in Bokaro handling things.

But then I figure the only thing to do is to burn the anger. So after a bit I continue my run, and finally run for an hour and forty minutes, and feel good about it.

I expected my father to visit that day, and he does visit me along with my local colleague from Bokaro, Ajay Dubey. As expected, they confirm my suspicions about how the legal process is going. My father says his expectation is another three to four days. I give him the letter for Vandita and tell him whom to call and also whom Vandita should call at the company to get things moving.

I realize that I really like coffee and I miss it. I don't miss cola or alcohol or anything as much. But a hot frothy coffee like they serve at the Prakash tea stall in Ambala Cantt. was really nice on a cold winter day.

———

Within two to three days of my arrival in jail, I had found a small broken steel glass, and had started keeping flowers in it. It is a simple routine—an activity, a distraction—to restock my broken steel glass vase with flowers. After a couple of days even Mukur gets into the act. Occasionally even he would add a rose or two to the glass. I do not like to pluck the roses from the bushes but never stop him.

There is also mustard growing wild inside the prison which has bright yellow flowers, and that is what I mostly keep in my 'vase'. The flowers last a few days in water. I usually change them every two to three days.

On a clear day, the early morning rays of the sun slant into the room and fall directly on the flowers, and for a brief minute or two they look radiant. Gives me something beautiful to look forward to each morning.

9 January 2013

Today is my day off from running. I decide to take it easy and read my book tucked into my warm blanket until I absolutely have to leave the bed.

One of the people in the ward who is increasingly noticeable, and sometimes for the wrong reasons, is Akhilesh, the deeply religious teacher I mentioned in the 'victim' category earlier on.

Akhilesh is as visibly religious as it gets. He has a heavy beard. He smears yellow 'haldi' on both earlobes and also his neck. Before specific activities he wraps his 'janeu' (sacred thread worn across the torso) around his ear. For prayers he changes into a pure saffron garment. He has established his own praying area in the temple space, with his god-picture set up with a different orientation than the rest of the temple. He is very particular that nobody should touch his personal god picture. However, since most of this does not impact anyone else in any way, people are largely happy to ignore it. His appearance, along with his reputation for prayer had earned him the nickname 'pujari' (priest) in the entire jail. Even though he rarely steps out of the hospital ward, anything remotely unusual is hot news amongst the bored inmates, and spreads fast. On occasion people would refer to him as the '*chela*' (student) and to Reiki Chacha as his guru, which he does not like at all and vehemently denies. The sense I get is that he does not think too highly of Reiki Chacha.

Akhilesh would pray in two spells—one three-odd hour spell in the morning, and then another three to four hours in the evening. This initially does not bother anyone. But after the initial few days he starts expecting the ward residents to make very little noise so that he does not get disturbed. This is still okay in the morning as most men step out into the sunlight. In the evening after lock-down it is pretty hard to be quiet—20 men locked into a single room, and often there is no power. There would be nothing to do but talk or play ludo or cards or some such, and any such activity inevitably means some amount of noise.

At times Akhilesh would stay seated in his corner and loudly click his fingers or even clap his hands to indicate to people to keep it down. Mostly, the prisoners would quiet down on the signal. But on one occasion when clapping his hands did not work, he burst out loudly—still sitting in lotus position. Akhilesh's tirade is turning into an argument with one particular prisoner when he himself withdraws and decide to drop it.

I think that asking 15 people to stay quiet so that one man can pray is a bit much. And none of the prisoners make a racket on purpose—it is just their nature. But since I am rarely the one making noise I am able to quietly watch the whole situation from a distance.

Akhilesh would often start his prayers in the morning, and on the days I was not out running, I would be in bed reading my book when he started. A few days ago he was sitting in the lotus position and needed his 'prasad'—the food which is offered to God as part of prayer. The prasad is in a plastic jar about 4 feet from him, but a lot further from me. He calls out to me—I am in bed in my warm blanket reading my book—and asks if I could hand him the prasad. I do and go back to my reading.

Today is a severely cold morning, and I plan to not run but stay in bed and enjoy reading my book to the hilt. My double blanket is cosy and the cold air and light coming in from the window makes it perfect. In the Churchill book, Rommel has reappeared, and has just started his campaign across Libya, and the British are on the run. In fact, he is also turning Italians into decent soldiers with his leadership! Just then Akhilesh asks me to hand him his prasad again. I am deep in my book, snug in my cosy blanket. I do not move—but call out to Raju to hand him the jar (which Raju does not do—Raju does not like Akhilesh as they have argued a couple of times) and continue with my reading. Akhilesh finally gets up himself and grabs the jar, and goes back to his prayer.

My opinion is that just because you're pursuing your interest, and it involves religion and rituals, does not make it more important than my interest that I am pursuing. Not to me anyway. But somewhere Akhilesh expects everyone to keep him on a pedestal because of the hours he sits in worship.

Time c-r-a-w-l-s in this place. No running today so the day seems even longer. Stayed in bed and read my book till 9 a.m. Then wash up. I go to the library and read the paper. Then stroll around and change the flowers in my broken steel glass vase. Then read. Then write a bit. Then do some freehand exercises. Have lunch at 11.30 a.m. Then read more. Then stroll some more. Now sitting in the clinic and writing.

10 January 2013

Start the day with a one-hour run. Have run out of all the goodies and snacks except a few cookies and oranges. Don't feel like asking for anything more because I am hoping tomorrow is my last day here. I spend the morning sitting in the sun reading my book. Then I step out for a bit, and meet up with Pappu who is sunning himself in the courtyard with one of his brothers. We chat generally about the Bokaro real estate market, and about one of the bigger Bokaro builders who is also in this jail, and lives in Ward 9. He gives me a few property investment tips, but I don't know if I really want any long-term attachments to Bokaro.

The one thing I can safely say is that if one had to choose a time to be in jail, this was probably the very best time. Comfort comes from warmth, which can be arranged with warm clothes and blankets. Sitting in the sun is nice. Running is easy. Mosquitoes are easier to handle as one is largely covered.

On the other hand, summer in this place would be a nightmare. With the erratic power supply even fans would not be dependable, mosquitoes would abound, and disease would also be rampant. The only advantage of the summer would be the longer days and the shorter lock-down duration.

———

Two men from the neighbouring ward are released today. One of them, when he got back from the court yesterday, could not stop crying—he had been released after 18 months in jail. If after 18 months in jail someone is released as innocent, what does that mean? Why hold someone whose guilt is in question in prison for so long? Not even grant bail?

And how does he now get back to a normal life? Any profession: a job or a business or even an education would be severely—probably terminally—disrupted by something like this. If you had a job, and you go back looking for work, how do you explain the gap? Do you say you were in jail? Even if you are proven innocent, would anyone hire such a person? Would I?

———

There are two ways to leave this jail. One is that the prisoner is freed: either the court decides in his favour, or he is let out on bail.

The other is when the prisoner is convicted, and is then sent to the jail for convicts. The big central jail in Hazaribagh, which is supposed to have 3000 prisoners, many of whom are hardened criminals. So far I have only heard of releases—never heard of the transfer to the bigger, scarier jail.

Wonder if it is simply because such convictions haven't happened, or because people choose not to talk about them.

11 January 2013

Early morning I wake up to the slow realization that I am still in jail. Just 10 minutes ago I was laughing hysterically along with my brother because we had mangled some song lyrics into really funny words, which I cannot remember now in the awake world.

I am hoping for release today—just hadn't realized how much. My father visited me again today after two days. His skillset is how to be honest upright army officer. And he can fix battle tanks. Neither is a skillset that works in the Jharkhand legal system. He has been working tirelessly to get me out. He has also told me of the stories, which are quite ghastly, about the false promises everyone has made him about how they will get me out. Hollow assurances given by people who don't mean a word they say. He also told me about the incident where he visited a police station—which looked like a scrap dealer's shop—only to find the seniormost cop there so drunk that he could not even walk straight. Evidently this happened on the night of 24 December itself, but he thought it would not be right to share it with me during our very first meeting.

The news he carried today is no better. Evidently, my release order could have been given yesterday, but some paper committed for the morning was delayed and now everything has to go into next week—probably Wednesday, because Monday is a holiday in court.

I have been in here for 18 days now—stupidly and unjustly. I don't know what the Everonn people are doing. Nobody is here on the ground: my father is the only reason I have any hope or information. The lawyers seem to do whatever they please, and absolutely nobody seems to own responsibility for my release.

After I meet my father I come back, lie in bed, cover my face with my blanket and cry my eyes out. I haven't really properly cried ever since this whole circus started. After crying, I rage—in my mind—with all the anger I can vent, against my boss for being so callous and indifferent to the fact that I am in jail—unjustly, unfairly, and only because I work for him! The most irritating is the fact that nobody from the company seems to be involved in what is happening in the courts every day.

I am not sure exactly when I drift off to sleep. I wish there is some way I could sleep for five straight days, and wake up only when it is time to get out!

***

After I wake up I go out, sit and chat with Nageshwar. He has been here for a total of seven years in two spells, for the same case. In between, when he got out for a bit he got married (a second time—his first wife is dead) and had a baby girl. But he was arrested soon after she was born, and has been in jail for the past four years. His daughter is now four and a half years old. He shows me her picture from when she was three months old. It is the only picture he has. My daughter is the same age. I start to tell him what a great age this is, and how kids are just so adorable and loving at this age. But then I bite my tongue. He's been here for almost her entire childhood—he has no idea what it is like to be the father of a four-year-old. All I would do is hurt him.

As we are talking, Aseem walks in. Aseem is a cheeky, good-looking guy. He always has some joke or one-liner coming up, and likes to be the centre of attention. He is usually a cheerful presence. However, today he is really disturbed—the high court has rejected his bail plea for the next six months, saying that if the case is not resolved by then he could apply again. It has visibly shaken him. He digs out a cigarette and lights it while talking non-stop about going to the Supreme Court and so on. The certainty that he will be here for the next six months is obviously a huge disappointment.

I am still feeling low but there is no way I can talk about my five-day delay in being released as bad news in front of these two.

I again think it would be nice if I could have a drink tonight. It is possible for a price, but needs planning. I am wondering how to smuggle in some rum and coke. The only person I trust who can pull off something like that in my circle is Aseem. But when I try talking to him, he is just too tuned out because of his bail rejection. So my desire for a drink remains a desire yet again.

And to top it all, there is no afternoon tea today. The stated reason is because there is chicken for dinner. Like that makes any sense at all. Blast this place!

12 January 2013

Today I have decided to take things into my own hands.

This problem—my being in jail—is not my father's problem. It is not my family's problem. It is Everonn's problem. But the company is, conveniently, taking no ownership at all. Despite these ridiculous, repeated delays they still have nobody on the ground in Bokaro or Ranchi. The lawyers still seem to be doing as they please. I was first told that a release would happen by 7–8 January. Then 10–11 January. Now they are saying 15–16 January. I think they have to start taking some ownership for their promises.

I have eaten nothing since morning. Had two cups of tea, one orange, and one sip of water. My father visited me today along with some Everonn employee named Mahesh. Mahesh looked like he had just shat in his pants, and my father said that he was hesitating to come to the jail. And he works for the legal department of Everonn. Heaven help me!

Evidently, this is Mahesh's second visit to Bokaro—the previous visit was soon after my arrest, but he had not felt it was important to come and meet me then. In fact, only one person—one Ajay Shetty—had come and met me in jail. Ajay Dubey, my colleague from the Bokaro office, was the only person who really seemed to care about my plight, and was there through everything. Not one senior manager or official had felt the need to come and visit me as I rotted in jail. No Rakesh, no Anand, no Sunny, no Dino.

I tell my father and Mahesh the following things very specifically:

1. My father is to leave immediately for Delhi.
2. I am not going to accept any food or water from any outside source anymore.
3. Inside the prison I will stop eating. If at all I do, I will eat one small meal a day.
4. I will refuse to meet all visitors until they have arranged for my release. Meeting them and getting more false promises is pointless.

My dad has brought food and water with him but I send it back. Hate turning him away, but I explain things to him the best that I could.

I feel that my father's presence in Bokaro is acting as a cushion for the company. Everonn is actually delegating to my father, and expecting he will do the company's job. And between my father, my brother and my brother-in-law, they actually had been doing the company's job to a large extent.

The Bad Boys of Bokaro Jail

I want to change things so that nobody from my family is in Bokaro. Then my wife and my dad would call Everonn for daily updates. Everonn would not be able to provide any updates about me because I would refuse to meet anyone. And I would also have stopped eating, but would continue walking 3 to 4 hours a day, which would mean that in 10 to 15 days I would die and it would be Everonn's responsibility. So basically, I am hoping that the fact that I have stopped eating will make it a crisis for Everonn to get me out at the earliest.

Not that I want to die, but I just feel that if a serious crisis is not created for Everonn, then even the 15–16 January dates could easily move to 15–16 February or even March given the way they are going. And I am not ready to spend one minute more than I have to in Bokaro Jail.

Today I will complete 20 days in jail plus one day in the police station—21 days in captivity. The company could have arranged for my release in 14 days—I could have been free 5 days ago. The reason I am still here is that people talk big and forget to get things done. I am increasingly starting to see Everonn as the enemy here.

I am trying to be completely strategic and clear-headed as I do all this. I want to make sure that this is a very thought-through, clear-headed act on my part, and not something that actually causes me to start losing it.

That possibility becomes more real with the arrival of two new inmates yesterday. They had returned to the hospital ward after treatment at the mental hospital in Ranchi. One of them is called Anup.

When Anup and his friend arrived last night it was already dark, and there was no power. They were let into the ward by the cop well after sundown. As soon as Anup walks in he heads over to bed number one. I am in bed three, and bed two is vacant.

Raju sits with him. Anup asks Raju a lot of questions.

'Where has my bedsheet gone?'

'Where is XYZ *kaidi* (prisoner) now?'

And so on

He sounds like a very level-headed guy who is keen to catch-up on things in the ward. Clearly, he is very familiar with the ward, knows a lot of the older inmates, and also knows the rules. As he speaks to Raju, I cannot help notice his voice. It has a gentle, lyrical quality to it.

In a while, both Nageshwar and Aseem turn up. They both snigger and laugh a bit—obviously with reference to Aseem—and then tell me '*Uska tower chod diya hai.*' (He is a mental case). That is the tragic response in most such cases—the slightest deviation from normal, and people are branded as 'mad'.

Along with Aseem and Nageshwar, the power supply also returns. I get my first look at Anup—he is about 5 feet 6 inches, 'wheatish' complexion, and has a light stubbly beard. He has a squarish face and a small, upturned moustache. He walks with his chest—his whole abdomen, in fact—sticking out. For some reason his gait reminds me of Subhas Chandra Bose's gait. Although I have no clue how Subhas Chandra Bose actually walked, but in my mind, it would probably have been like the way Anup walks.

Anup asks Raju for a blanket. There are two kinds of blankets in the jail: the red one and the black one with a check pattern. The black ones are rougher and not as nice-looking: they are less premium. The red ones are softer and nicer-looking, and they are only available in the hospital ward. Raju hands Anup a black, check patterned blanket. Anup is upset. He says he wants a red one. He walks up and down the space between all the beds, and notices that many people are sleeping on the red blankets, that is, the blanket is being used as a bedsheet. This really upsets Anup and he immediately demands that everybody take their blankets out from underneath and use them only for covering themselves. Since he very forcefully asks everyone to do this, two red blankets become free and turn up on his bed.

But this has now become a crusade for Anup. He sees that Chaudhary (one of the ward residents—an amputee) is still sleeping on a red blanket. Anup wakes Choudhary up and insists that he get off the blanket. Initially, Choudhary just lies in bed and ignores Anup. The rest of the ward is watching. I try telling Anup that he already has two red blankets on his bed, but Nageshwar shakes his head, puts his finger on his lips to convey that I should stay quiet.

Anup continues standing right next to Chaudhary's bed and goes into a monologue: 'These blankets have been given by the government to take on top. To cover the bed you need to get sheets. Slowly, the prisoners have taken all the sheets away, and now none are left. Now if everyone uses blankets as sheets, what will people use to cover themselves? To save themselves from the cold? If two new patients come tomorrow what will they use? . . .' and so on he went.

Chaudhary finally says, 'Look, I am using this blanket as a sheet only because it is torn.'

Anup immediately says, 'Show me where it is torn. Even if it is torn I can use it to cover myself.'

That is the moment when Nageshwar jumps in—surprisingly reprimanding Choudhary. '*Arre*, you should listen to the man. What he is saying is right . . .'

And then he turns to Anup, 'What you are saying is right. Maybe he can give you the blanket in a bit? And look—there already are two red blankets on your bed!' With his hand Nageshwar quietly indicates to Choudhary to relax. Anup seems to have been distracted and pacified for the moment.

Just as we all think the situation was defused, Anup notices that Reiki Chacha is also using a red blanket as a sheet.

'You are also on a red blanket,' he says to Reiki Chacha abruptly. 'Take it out from underneath. It is not to be used like that.'

Reiki Chacha does not protest, and says, 'Okay, if that is how you want it . . .' but then both Nageshwar and Aseem jump in, saying, 'Look, he is an old man . . .' and so are able to dissuade Anup and move him along to his bed and his two precious blankets.

Aseem quickly changes the topic to dinner and asks whether or not Anup has eaten. Both Aseem and Nageshwar know Anup from earlier, and obviously know how to handle him. The trick seems to be never to confront or question him, but instead to give him a sense of power and then slowly divert his attention to something else.

13 January 2013

Happy Lohri! Today the festival of Lohri is celebrated up north where I come from. Had I been home I would have lit a fire, and friends would have come over. I would probably be drinking my favourite Scotch on ice. I love nothing better than a nice warm bonfire in the lawn on a cold winter night with close friends and some good music . . . it's been three weeks since any of the above.

In the jail, things have changed and my plan has gone into action. My father has left town, and my food intake is down to a fraction of before. All of yesterday and a lot of today all I have been able to think about is Everonn and the anger I feel. For hours together I have been cooking in this fire.

In fact, I haven't been for a run in four days, or bathed or shaved in three days. I have been feeling low, deceived and demotivated. I have tried reading but it is hard to focus on that as well. I just hope the people at Everonn start keeping their promises!

But today I remember Vandita's words from our last conversation. 'Be positive,' she said. 'Stay strong and take care of yourself.'

It is easy default behaviour to just boil in rage—especially since I am now perpetually hungry from consciously not eating. But I know she is right and that I cannot let the anger and hatred consume me. So I lay out a constructive plan: I decide to focus more on writing. Maybe look at more themes that I can write. Or maybe a different format. Maybe a short story? Or a poem? I also decide to check if the library has a dictionary. I am coming across some difficult words in my reading—going through a dictionary would be another way to kill time.

While I limit my food intake to one meal a day, I decide to continue to walk three to four hours every day and also do some freehand exercises every other day. I certainly want to look thinner and less healthy whenever I meet the Everonn people next—to make my threat of fasting credible. Yesterday, throughout the whole day all I ate was one orange and a light dinner. Today, breakfast is a glass of diluted milk, and lunch is half a banana. I have already walked an hour, and will walk another two hours in the afternoon. If only I had some music. When I am walking alone for hours and hours it is difficult to divert my mind from feeling anger at Everonn.

When the library opens, I go and look and actually find a dictionary there. It is thick but it is an English to Hindi dictionary, so it is rather basic and literal in the meanings it provides. Some of the stuff in it is just amazing. They have a few illustrations every few pages and one picture is of a zebra—except that under it is the description 'seahorse'. In another place a word is actually misspelt: yes, in a dictionary! Think twice before recommending the *Sahni Advanced English-English-Hindi Dictionary* to anybody. I will return it to the library tomorrow.

That day I also tell Dharmendar (Ghani's replacement in the kitchen) to stop sending me any special tea or food. No point ordering special food if I don't intend to eat anyway.

5.00 p.m.

So I walk another two hours in the afternoon. I am not feeling as strong because of the lack of food, but I push myself. I can see other people are able to perceive that my mood has changed. Both Nageshwar and Aseem have been especially thoughtful. Nageshwar tries to ensure that I eat every meal. Since I skipped lunch today and I am sitting and writing in the clinic, he sends Reiki Chacha in with some 'tilkut'—a super-sweet snack made of sesame seed and sugar.

As I walk I am joined by Pappu Ansari, again in his classic walking outfit of a lungi with a black leather jacket and bathroom slippers. The first thing he says is, 'You have been looking very down. Don't take too much tension. Things will work out eventually.' Words of comfort from someone who has been in prison for three months already, accused of murder. Not really that surprising. Murderers—alleged or otherwise—are also humans.

My friendship with Pappu becomes deeper the more we walk. Strangely, we hardly even meet or talk otherwise—I have never ever been to his ward, and he never visits mine. All our interaction happens when we are out walking. We have become walking partners of sorts over time. We chat about family and stuff. I tell him about how my wife, as well as my brother's wife, are both working women. He is pretty matter-of-fact, 'In small towns it is still rare, and in our community—Mohammedans—even less so. In my house I would not let my wife step out.'

'What about Hindu families in Bokaro?' I ask.

'There it is changing,' he replies 'But very slowly. Even women who work do only teaching jobs or work in banks and such.'

The big city versus small town chasm of India yawns before me.

'So do you have kids?' I ask him.

'No, I am not married yet. I was to get married in December, but then we got arrested in October.'

'So is the marriage still on?'

'Oh yes.' He uses the very charming Urdu work 'nikah' for marriage.

'Did your parents arrange it or did you fall in love?'

'Parents arranged it.'

He pauses, looks at me, smiles slightly sheepishly and adds, 'The girl that I loved married someone else.'

I smile back. 'It happens to the best of men.'

Although we come from very different worlds, it does

not prevent us from being able to form a connection. I think this is because neither of us tries to judge or change the other. We simply accept.

━━━━━

The most positive outcome of that walk, however, is an idea. I am still tied up in furious knots at the incompetence of Everonn, and the lack of concern evident from their actions. I want something more positive I can focus my energies on. While walking I think about my most positive experiences and I realize that my family is at the centre of it all. My amazing, amazing wife. And my two absolutely adorable kids—Anhad and Raahat. And as I think more about this I have this thought that the most positive thing for me to do at this stage would be to write down all my fond memories of both my kids. I decide that I would start a letter to each of my children which I would keep adding to and appending, and which I would finally hand over to them once they are grown up.

In these letters I would try and capture the precious past, every single memorable instance that I can remember with both of them. With the numerous years and so many memories to try and collect (my kids are four and six years), I would have a positive occupation for my time. More than that, I would create something that I, and hopefully they, would also truly and deeply cherish.

Ever since this idea has come to me everything seems to have changed. I am now actually looking forward to the next 3-4 days. Actually thinking I might go for a run. As I start thinking about the many small incidents I want to capture on paper and share with them, I cannot help but smile. There are too many tiny little things that fill my head. All filled with innocence. Many are about the adoration that kids at that tender age typically lavish upon their parents.

The change in my mood is actually incredible. Suddenly I do not feel so much hate for Everonn. Life is good again. The spring is back in my step.

14 January 2013

Today is Makar Sankranthi so the courts are closed. One additional day to spend in jail.

It is evidently a major festival in these parts. The day started with 'tilkut' again—which is so sweet that I cannot eat more than a little bit at a time. We are all served a 'special treat' of dahi (yogurt), chiwda (flattened rice), gur (raw sugar) and also sabzi. I decide to eat the meal as it is different food, and dahi is a rarity in the prison. I have a decent-sized meal after many days, although for me it does not live up to the hype. Makar, one of my two helpers in the ward—shares that it is his birthday today and that he had completed 20 years. That is why he is named Makar (after Makar Sankranthi). Unlike many Indian holidays, Makar Sankranti is fixed on the Christian calendar and so comes on the same date every year—14 January.

Makar is a strapping young man—dark, clean-shaven and well built. He is soft-spoken, and a helpful, gentle soul. One can regularly see him help Mahto-da up or down the steps, or generally help people in other ways.

On talking to him I realize that his aspirations are the same as those of any young middle-class youth. He just wants a good future, and a simple life with a happy family. And he seems quiet and industrious, and a willing worker. He has completed high school, and that should certainly help him move ahead—at least compared to other people like Raju. He is also in prison in a dowry-related case, but thankfully, in his case the wife is alive and well, and he has been accused of harassment. That means even if convicted his sentence will be much shorter than in a dowry-death case. Talking to him, of course, he sounds completely innocent. My guess is that—as in many such cases—he is in jail not because of his actions, but because of his inability to prevent the actions of his family towards his wife.

Today I start the process of writing the letters to my children, Anhad and Raahat. The process does distract me and helps me stay focused on the positive. It also reminds me a lot of my family though, and on occasion makes me cry. But overall it is a positive activity, and one that I enjoy a lot.

Just as I start feeling better and a little more cheerful, there is an announcement that I should come to the office. Two men from Everonn are there to meet me— including the company legal representative—Ajay—who had promised me that I would be out on 7 or 8 January. I have no desire to meet them, but in the announcement over the PA system, they did not say I had visitors. Just that I should come to the office.

As soon as I see the pair of them I want to leave. I am standing in the corridor when they approach me—the moment I see them I tell the guard to let me back into the jail where they cannot follow. As they come closer I tell them that I do not want to meet them or talk to them. Ajay starts to say, 'But Chetan . . .' but I cut him short.

'I don't want to talk to you. Have you secured my release?'

'No.'

'You are a liar and you are incompetent. You have repeatedly made promises you have not kept. I don't want any more false promises. I don't want to meet or talk to anyone until my release has been secured. Until then you do what you have to and I will do what I have to.' With that I turn and leave, and the gate is locked behind me.

For the next few hours I cannot get the incident out of my head. Again, the scenes of confrontation keep playing in my head—the things I would say to the HR head and to the head of legal affairs. *Man, I could hit somebody! Aaaarrgh!!*

Have to snap out of it. If I let the anger keep a hold on me, it is a self-perpetuating cycle. I had just about managed to shake it off, and now it is back. I am looking for any distraction I can find, and Nageshwar offers me one—although a rather grim one. He asks me—rather hesitantly—if I could translate his court judgement into the Hindi language. I agree and so he hands me a document of some 20-odd pages. We start off—me telling him the meaning of each sentence in Hindi, and he writing the meaning down. Pretty soon it becomes too tedious, and he suggests that I first explain the meaning to him page by page. So I read through the entire document and explain what is there on each page to him.

The picture isn't pretty. Nageshwar's wife had been found dead in their house one morning, one and a half years after their wedding. Her family had claimed that a TV and a motorcycle had been demanded in addition to the dowry already given. They claimed that since her family had not met these demands, Nageshwar and his mother had killed his wife.

Nageshwar's version is different. He says that his wife had been miserable from the very first day of their marriage. He said she was from a better-off family in the city of Bokaro, and she had to move to his village, which was without electricity or running water. She had to cook food on firewood and dung cakes. She was very unhappy in the village and so had committed suicide.

The key evidence in all such cases is always the medical report. The court judgement said that a 7-foot-long piece of rope was found next to the body. Nageshwar's defence claimed this was used by her to commit suicide. However, the post-mortem report—which was also included in the judgement—clearly said that the medical facts point towards murder and not suicide.

Nageshwar maintains his innocence and says it was genuinely suicide. He says his wife was truly miserable with her life in the village. I think there are some pretty loose ends but do not want to get into being a judge. That would involve asking too many uncomfortable questions. Nageshwar is already in jail—and has been for the past seven years. Going deeper would achieve nothing.

Nageshwar claims that his wife's family paid off the medical officer, and had the medical report doctored. So he wants me to now help translate the medical report section of the judgement only. Stuff like 'horigental grooved ½' wide mark with ecchomised and abraded . . .' and 'Blood mixed with frothy discharge at nostril.' It is not my idea of a fun read. Despite the terrible English, the medical jargon and the gore, it is still better than seething within about Everonn for days. At least it is some kind of work and may help a possibly innocent man. Though it is also a pretty certain way of losing one's appetite.

15 January 2013

I slept after 10 p.m. last night but am up at 4 a.m., unable to sleep. I toss and turn, fighting mosquitoes and my demons at the same time. Finally get out of bed at 6.15 a.m. and decide to go for a run—the one thing I can still choose to do in a place with few choices. Change my clothes. Stretch. Then the cop comes at unlocking time, says there is a talaashi, lets Aseem out and locks everyone else back in. So much for choices. I do some freehand exercises, and then read my book. Finally we are unlocked after 7.30. The mood to run is gone, and so I walk for an hour.

I have been watching Anup carefully over the last three days. Besides the one blanket incident, he seems to have settled in well and seems perfectly normal. He seems to have an amazing ability to sleep—but that could be because of the medication he is on. I had asked him if he liked it better in the hospital at Ranchi or here. He said he prefers the jail better.

Aseem has an irritating habit of trying to have a laugh at other people's expense. He tried to incite Anup yesterday, saying Chaudhary and Reiki Chacha were still sleeping on the red blankets. Anup simply answered, 'I asked them, but if they don't remove their blankets what can I do?'

In casual conversation, Anup tells me that he has already spent five years behind bars. He is in for a dowry-death case as well. When I ask about his family, he says nobody comes to visit him.

———

Jail does have a culture of its own, and I don't think it is very particularly a criminal culture. I think it is simply a Jharkhand small-town culture. Lower-middle class in its flavour.

There is still a significant distance that generations maintain here. For example, there are many things that sons do not do before their elders. It is true for me as well but in a much smaller way. But I think it is much stronger and more pronounced here. Pappu Ansari and his two brothers live in Ward 2 while his father and two uncles live in Ward 10 (the Roja ward). He said that he felt that everyone is more comfortable this way. It is not that his brothers do anything blasphemous like drinking. They are all teetotallers. But they just feel that they have to watch themselves a lot less, and are also able to smoke more comfortably if they live in a different ward.

Another aspect which I initially found shocking, but have increasingly come to accept as 'normal' is the difference in the attitude toward women and their rights.

People here believe that women are very clearly and unequivocally inferior to men, and should be kept in their place. Even to the gang-rape story the response has not been as black-and-white as in my 'CNN-IBN' bubble. So when the Madhya Pradesh industry minister Kailash Vijayvargiya talks about a '*Lakshman rekha* that women should not cross', most men nod their head in agreement.

There is a case where a man had been arrested along with a bunch of other men as the rape accused. However, this one guy is supposed to be the victim's boyfriend and said he is wrongly accused as he had never raped her. The victim had evidently come to meet her boyfriend in jail a few times on her 'scooty'—and it was seen as extremely inappropriate behaviour by everyone in the jail.

On top of that she had assured him that she would arrange for his release! Such audacity in a woman!!

It is also interesting to see the difference in the English and the Hindi newspapers—especially the more local Hindi dailies. The indignation that an English daily paper express about someone making a chauvinistic statement— say about the gang-rape case—may simply be a factual statement being quoted without judgement in the Hindi one.

Clearly, the role of the newspapers here is not as much to change opinions as to reinforce existing opinions. Makes it that much easier to sell.

There is a whole cycle of interests that drive the information and opinion cycles. The newspapers have clearly defined audiences, and no paper wants to be seen as preaching, so everyone tries to toe the line and stay well within the mainstream of local opinion to be able to sell the most number. That doesn't matter if you sell soap, but as a journalistic entity, competition of this nature actually is a bad thing—it helps stick with old ways of thinking. It is actually a negative force, because while every newspaper provides the same information, the press is afraid to have a strong opinion because of the fear that too many people may disagree (and consequently, move to a less forward-thinking newspaper). So all Hindi dailies stick with the mainstream opinion of their audience, which is safe.

This is unfortunate as there is very strong power and credibility that the written word carries. But most people stay happy in their closed loop of self-affirming sources of information and opinions.

No, it is not all gloom and doom—things have overall improved significantly from the past, with people having more choice and more points of view being available. However, the balls required to be a newspaper with integrity and conviction is what seems to be completely lacking today, and that is a big loss, especially in a democracy.

Another aspect inherent to the culture is the level of intrusiveness people demonstrate. At least that is what I think it is initially. I would be walking and someone I barely know would ask, '*Naha liya?*' (Had your bath?) by way of greeting.

In the jail there is only cold water for a bath, and I am here in peak winter, so I have typically been bathing only every other day (with the exception of days earmarked for running). So in the early days my response to the bath question would be something factual like 'Not taking a bath today', which was eventually simplified to 'Not yet'.

But I have also realized that the salutation is not meant to be an intrusion. It is almost a greeting like 'All well?' But the expectation seems to be that everyone has a bath every day.

Similarly, one day the lawyer, whom I had met just once, suggested, 'Why don't you dye your hair?'

'My hair doesn't bother me. Does it bother you?' I retorted. Maybe it was a little too rough, so I added with a smile, 'I am already married so I don't have to impress any girls. Now I am in jail—not too much point dyeing my hair, is there?'

On another occasion I was standing in a group with my notebooks under my arm (the notebooks which contain all my precious writing). There was hardly anyone I really knew in the group. Without feeling the need to ask, this one guy conversationally said, 'Let us see what you are writing in these' and started to take the notebooks from me. I held firm and told him, 'These are not for sharing.'

'*Arre*, what is the big deal? Let me see,' he said, and continued to tug at the notebooks.

I don't even know this guy's name!

'No,' I say, emphatically.

He lets go. He does not look offended, but rather perplexed—as though he just doesn't get it.

One of the new prisoners has brought a ludo board so it is a new activity. We played three hours of ludo last evening in the ward. Time flies. Don't know when 5.30 became 8.30 p.m. I don't think I have ever enjoyed ludo so much before.

16 January 2013

I am on Facebook, and people from all over are popping up on chat and asking how I am and when I got back. My phone rings incessantly. Vandita and the kids are also sitting around me looking at my laptop screen. We're all smiling. Suddenly the word 'jora' penetrates through the haze and the heavy iron latch clangs loudly as it is opened. Welcome to day 23 in jail!

Ajay Dubey from Everonn came to meet me today. He is a good guy—one of the key staff members from the Bokaro office. I met him because he is probably the only person from the Gems-Everonn group who has not lied to me or given me any false hope. More importantly, he genuinely seems interested in my well-being. He has come to meet me and also brought food to the jail on multiple occasions, although he does not have to.

Today he has come alone, as he knows I may refuse a meeting if Ajay Shetty was also there. He has brought food for me, which I refuse. I am eating more than one meal a day now—but still don't feel like eating three square meals.

He gives me an update on the legal front. The company has finally told Ajay Shetty, the lawyer who works with the mother company—Gems Education in Dubai—to base himself in Bokaro. This is 17 days after my imprisonment. From Ajay Dubey's understanding the bail order is likely for 21 January now.

Yet another extension on the date. I am livid, and I don't hide my feelings from Ajay Dubey. He, of course, can do nothing about it. He insists repeatedly that I take the food he has brought, but I refuse. Finally, he leaves.

After his departure I am called back into the office. This time the superintendent wants to meet me.

The superintendent is the most senior person in the jail. He is a nice, helpful man and has treated me as a 'special case' ever since my father's first visit. He allows my visitors the exception of being able to visit me during non-visiting hours, and we are allowed to sit in a room and talk, instead of shouting to each other from behind a wire mesh.

When the superintendent meets me he asks me how I am, and advises me that I should review all legal papers and keep myself informed of all that is happening in court. He says it is unfortunate and unjust and so on. But, by this point, I have become fundamentally indifferent.

I tell him that everyone from Everonn has either lied to me or is incompetent. I also tell him that I only trust Ajay Dubey, and that I am resigned to being in jail forever. I do not want to meet anybody because people give dates which mean nothing and hope is repeatedly broken. The superintendent says that resigning from the process would not help. But I tell him that from inside the prison and in my current state of mind I cannot try and manage things. I will do what I have to once I am out.

He suggests that I keep myself busy. I tell him that my main pastime is reading and that I am on my last book, and am also sick of playing ludo (both true). He suggests that I read books from the library, and I tell him I have already checked out the two English books there.

I guess he realizes that the conversation is not going anywhere, and since he is repeatedly hitting a wall, he ends our conversation by asking me if everything is all right inside. I am tempted to tell him that is a stupid question. Instead, I say yes.

Later, Aseem tells me that the reason for calling me back was to ask me to eat the food Ajay Dubey had brought for me. But I guess after our conversation, the superintendent had decided against bringing it up. Good.

This imprisonment has helped me reflect upon and realize the difference between a principled, ethical employer who gets things done, and those that talk. I have now worked for both kinds.

I have worked for strong organizations such as the Tata group and MNCs like Ogilvy & Mather. For both the above I can say with 100 per cent confidence that in a similar situation the company would have stood by and fought for the employee from day one, and ensured his release at the very earliest instance. Not just an individual, an entire task-force would have set up camp in Bokaro and taken ownership of the process.

I have myself, on one occasion as the CEO of a small company, spent four hours in a police station because one of my employees was attacked. Although nobody was hurt, I insisted that an FIR be filed because I wanted a clear message to go out that such behaviour towards any employee would not be tolerated. Everyone in the company knew I had taken this stand. The behaviour, conviction and actions of the leader determine how people in any company feel and act. Such actions define to the employees how the company views them, and how valued and protected they are. It lets them know whether, in a crisis, the company will stand by them, or whether it will abandon and possibly abuse them.

The fact that no senior manager—neither the acting CEO, nor Mr Sunny Varkey, the owner, felt any need to travel to Bokaro even once to meet me or understand what is happening on the legal front in person said a lot to me. They had tried to manage things over the phone, and after seventeen days had finally decided to place one individual in Bokaro. To me, sitting in jail, all this is an irresponsible outrage of the highest order. But even to the mass of Everonn employees it will say a lot. It tells them how much they are valued, and how much the company will care for them in a crisis. It defines not just what the company will do for them, it also defines how much they should stick their neck out for the company. It lets them know how much passion and personal involvement to bring to their work.

From a neutral and purely leadership perspective, I think this is a huge opportunity lost for Everonn. The company is currently emerging from a crisis, and has a workforce which is very demotivated and uncertain about the future. The Gems group of Dubai had taken control a little over a year back. However, in over one year of ownership it had not been able to bring about any noticeable change to operations and business on the ground. A lot of promises had been made. But not enough were kept, and too many broken. The company continued in a state of limbo of sorts, and with the continued uncertainty many good people left. Then, to effect a serious change, the Gems group brought on board a senior advisor, who in turn brought me in to join the senior team in October. And in December I was arrested.

The two critical things for Everonn to manage at this point were:

1. How quickly the employee in prison is released
2. How the business interest of Everonn in Bokaro is handled

The company had the opportunity to demonstrate intent, confidence and a new, changed leadership. Positive, effective handling of the situation would have spoken more loudly to the employees than any words ever could. However, Everonn faltered on both the above fronts. Not only has Everonn been unable to secure a prompt release for me, it has also not effectively handled the situation on the ground at Bokaro. The centre will eventually shut down if things continue at this rate. Since the company did not execute, this incident will also fall into a familiar pattern of lost battles and broken promises that the employees are used to seeing. This especially undermines the new management, and leaves it with no credibility.

Everonn is like a losing fighter in a boxing match. There was a brief opportunity to land a flurry of blows on the opponent and get back in the reckoning. Instead, the fighter let his guard down, and took a further beating.

Pity.

17 January 2013

I finished the refill in one of my two pens today. Don't remember the last time that happened to me.

———

Vandita came to see me today. She flew from Delhi to Ranchi and reached the jail around 2 p.m.

I am called into the office and am just so astounded to see her! Thankfully, we are allowed to meet and talk in private. I just hold her close to me and cling to her for sooo sooo long. It is just so amazing to have her in my arms. She probably thinks I look terrible. I haven't shaved in a week—don't see the point anymore when I am inside the jail.

She tells me about all that is happening as far as the case is concerned, and how the company has pushed the court date from 16 January to the 21st to be '100 per cent certain' that my release would happen.

Evidently, the company had refunded every one of the complainants, and is in the process of obtaining affidavits from them all, saying they had no further claims. She said that of the 83 complainants, 76 had signed affidavits. This is the same number I had heard yesterday from Ajay Dubey.

I ask her how come the number had not become 83 yet, and she says that the company felt that 76 is 'enough'. I don't get it. If the whole purpose of pushing the date out is to be '100 per cent certain' then why were they stopping at less, yet again? Especially when the shortfall is so small, and they have four full days in hand! I am amazed at how the company continues to be so lax about things.

I tell Vandita to take it up in no uncertain terms with the company.

Whenever the company had been asked (by my father or wife) about the reason for the delay in my release and why nothing is happening, the company management had frequently talked about some conspiracy theory—that someone is actively acting against us, that there were vested interests. But the more I saw and thought about the way things were being done, the more I am convinced that the 'conspiracy theory' is just an attempt to deflect the blame from the company's own incompetence.

Anyway, I have to consciously try and not think too much about Everonn. The amount of anger I feel is very unlike me. I think it is overall depressing and also damaging for me, and I continue to try not to think about it—as much as possible.

Besides the case, of course, I asked Vandita how the kids are and if they had also come. She said that she had left them at a close relative's place back in Gurgaon. They are really little—four and six years—so cannot be without either parent for too long.

She said that she talked to my son—Anhad—before coming to Bokaro and told him that she was going away for two days to meet me. He said, 'You don't go—otherwise like Papa you will also go for two days and not come back.' That made me choke on my tears.

Anyway, she had finally convinced him and she is now in Bokaro for two days, till tomorrow. Bokaro is not the kind of place where she would be comfortable staying alone in a hotel, so she is staying at Ajay Dubey's house.

She tells me about how all our friends have pitched in to help from day one. How practically everyone is aghast at the inordinate delay as the general information everyone has is that getting bail is just a two-or -three-day-long process.

The kids had resumed school after the initial few days they missed. She told me how one morning Raahat—my four-year-old daughter—woke up in the morning with her thumb in her mouth and said, 'Mummy, I am missing Papa.' She told me about how concerned—and how helpless—the whole family felt.

I just felt so much better after Vandita's visit. I have begun to hope again that if a favourable decision is given on the 21st then I can be out by the 22nd. And I do not feel as isolated as earlier. Plus I have Vandita's visit tomorrow to look forward to. I decide to go for a run the next morning.

—————

Once back inside, the news is that Reiki Chacha's bail has been approved today, so he will be out tomorrow. While he does talk a bit too much, he will be missed. Overall, he is a positive, pleasant presence and entertaining in his own way.

18 January 2013

I am up since 4 a.m. tossing and turning. At 5.15, I finally dig out my book and start reading. Volume III of the history of the Second World War by Churchill is more gripping than the first two volumes—almost a page-turner! I finally get out of bed at 6.35 a.m. and fly out of the gates the instant they open. Run for an hour, and follow-up with some freehand exercises. I want to get my beard shaved off now. I had asked Vandita about the beard, and she had not said anything except that it had a lot of grey. But I had asked her specifically how I looked and her response was not too convincing.

But my beard now is too thick for me to shave off myself. I have just one razor, and that is also at the end of its life. I did not expect to be in here this long! And the jail barber is just too busy today. Maybe the beard will have to stay: once she leaves I will, again, have little reason to shave it off.

I am bathed and ready at 9 a.m. I want to be ready when Vandita comes. She finally turns up at 1.20 p.m. and we talk for over an hour. I think it is one of the most pleasant times I have had in jail. All other visitors had only been for updates on the case etc. But I had not had a good long conversation with anyone in a month. It is so great to meet her. She also gives me the letter she had been writing. One of them mentions how after 15 years of marriage we were back to having 'supervised visits'. Hadn't thought of it like that!

Vandita has brought some food, bottled water and stuff that I had asked for. She has also brought a pen—which is desperately needed. And she has brought me a book, a collection of Mirza Ghalib's poetry, of which I am a big fan. I am looking forward to digging deeper into that. One of the couplets—which rings completely true to me in here—is:

'*Runj se khuger hua insan to mit jata hai runj*
Mushkilein mujh per padein inti ki asaan ho gaien'
(Once a human becomes habituated to sorrow, then sorrow goes away
I have faced so many hardships that they all became easy)

On top of everything else, Vandita also brought four bars of Cadbury's Fruit & Nut. It feels like going from hunger to gluttony in one stroke!

She tells me that someone from the press is interested in my story. I think about it—it would not reflect very positively on the company. I tell her not to talk to the press just yet, but that if things did not happen on Monday as promised then she should. But I just desperately, desperately hope that Monday's hearing will be in my favour.

———

After she leaves I come back to the ward with my packets of goodies. The letters that she has written are the first priority. They will be read over and over, of course. After that I eat some biscuits.

One more thing I had asked Vandita for was a chessboard. I had played ludo for a couple of days and rapidly lost interest, but it made me realize how much fun board games can be. However, after getting the chessboard, I realize that hardly anyone in the ward knows how to play chess. Not only do most prisoners not know how to play, they also have no desire to learn. Only Akhilesh knows how to play and so we play a couple of games. I am not an expert at the game but we have some good games. Although I lose both, I am quite absorbed, and it helps pass another hour.

———

Ghani is back as the kitchen-in-charge since the past two or three days, so I guess a new deal has been struck between him and the Zamindar. The food quality goes back to 'bad' within hours of his reinstatement.

19 January 2013

Last night is the first time that I sleep through most of the night. I do wake up once because some recorded bhajan starts playing, and because a bright light is on somewhere.

I blink and remove the blanket from my face to find the light on and Nageshwar reading. It is 4.30 a.m. I give him my booklight and ask if I can turn off the light. He readily agrees.

I lie down in bed after turning the light off, and actually fall back to sleep. Wake up to the calls of 'jora'. I do not run today but walk a good distance. In the afternoon, Akhilesh asks if I want to play chess. I am writing, but agree and we play two games. As we play, I notice Anup watching us. I ask if he knows how to play and he nods.

After two games with Akhilesh, I ask Anup if he would like to play. He nods. We have just started the game when after a few moves he says, '*Hum thoda fresh ho ke aayen?*' (Can I just use the bathroom?)

'Now? Maybe we can finish the game?' I suggest.

'Lots of pressure,' he says matter-of-factly.

'Okay,' I shrug. It's not like I have a busy appointment calendar.

He immediately gets up, changes out of his trousers into his lungi, grabs some soap and rushes off. In a while he comes back, changes again into his trousers and we resume.

He beats me squarely at chess. Somehow I had assumed that since he is a psychiatric case he would not be a good player. In fact when I had suggested to Akhilesh that he play a game with Anup he had laughed and said no. But Anup is a good player. He opened both games very well, and eventually won both the games we played.

My flawed assumption is flung in my face, and that is quite a revelation to me. Just because Anup has a condition does not mean he isn't smart. Makes me think of John Nash. Sure, the man was a schizophrenic, but he also won the Nobel Prize. The same applies to Anup. Maybe he has a mental ailment, but that did not make him any less smart.

My name is on the court list again today. Having seen the reality last time, I have no desire to go a second time. I request Nageshwar to help and he puts me down as sick so I am spared the ordeal. Getting by with a little help from my friends.

After lock-up today evening we have a snack—mixing *namkeen* with *murmure* to increase the quantity. While chatting, Mahto-Da tells us how last night '*Nageshwar ka bhi tower chod diya*' (Nageshwar is losing it). He says that Nageshwar is comfortable in a 'steady state' and keeps himself busy and content in the jail. But every time he gets a visitor it throws everything out of gear for him.

Now his being awake at 4.30 a.m. made sense. I had also overheard him in the clinic yesterday telling someone 'I don't deserve this. I don't know why I am here. God has mysterious ways that I don't understand.' Except he did not sound particularly devotional. He sounded quite pissed off.

20 January 2013

Today is the day of the Standard Chartered Mumbai Marathon. My wife and I are registered for the full marathon, and have trained for months for this race. I was pretty certain that I would be out by now—one of the reasons to run in here was to train for this race. But it's been 29 days and I am still here. I think only a runner can understand what this really means!

My sleep last night was broken and intermittent. I could see that Nageshwar is still not sleeping normally. It is warmer now—not as cold as it was two weeks back. The number of flies and mosquitoes seems to have increased. I run to the loo as soon as the cell door is unlocked—my stomach has been a little iffy since yesterday. I really hope I do not fall ill.

The ward next to ours—the juvenile ward—has a small 14-inch black and white TV. The antenna is improvised by cutting a metal sieve at one end and hanging it from a wall. Two wires connect the 'antenna' to the TV.

Consequently a grey, grainy image appears on the TV when switched on. Not many people watch it. The viewership peaks whenever there is a cricket match, though. Like yesterday when there was an India–England one-day cricket match at Ranchi. It was that much more interesting to people in the jail because it was happening in the same state.

The aspect I enjoy most of the TV is the music. The TV also doubles up as an FM player, and the kids in the juvenile ward often have it playing loud as early as 6 a.m. Every once in a while I hear one of my favourite songs on it. 'Kitne dafe' or 'Dhoom pichuk' or 'Pehli baar mohabbat ki hai'. One morning I heard 'Tu hi mera mera mera'. It reminded me of a parody that my wife had made which went 'Tu hi mara mara mara'. Ironic that it had come true. Made me smile.

The doctor also visits again today and a long line of prisoners forms to see him, and he disposes of it in record time. I am a little apprehensive that he might come into the ward and ask what my ailment is, but fortunately he does not. While he pays his mood-based visit to the jail, the cures he offers are very suspect. And he clearly doesn't care about health inside the prison. Nothing is done about prevention.

So the overwhelming presence of flies and mosquitoes is not surprising. When the power fails after lock-up (and the music next door also stops) each evening, one can hear a hum of mosquitoes loud enough to fill the room.

Similarly, flies are rampant. In fact, I have now stopped collecting flowers because they attract so many flies. I am amazed and a little bothered by Anup's ability to sleep with flies on his face. I guess he has just adapted to their presence. Maybe I have too, and just don't know it!

21 January 2013

I have been up since 5 a.m., tossing and turning. Between the Odomos and my gamchha I am able to keep the mosquitoes at bay. But I just cannot sleep past 5 o'clock. Judgement Day! Yet again.

Yesterday morning I had changed into my running clothes and stepped out, but just did not feel like it so came back to bed and read my book. Walked a couple of hours, though.

Today I have decided to be fully limbered-up and ready before the gate opens so that I can start running immediately as soon as I am outside. Haven't run for the three days since Vandita left so time to kick it back in.

———

Aseem was telling me last night about the time in 2010 when Ravi Shankar had visited the jail. I was quite surprised: they had got Ravi Shankar to do a sitar concert inside the jail! Wow!!

But as I asked more questions I realized that it was not Ravi Shankar the sitar maestro—in fact Aseem did not even know that someone named Ravi Shankar is a famous sitar player. Aseem had been talking about 'Sri Sri Ravi Shankar', the godman.

For some strange reason some U2 lyrics rang out in my head:

'Have you come here for forgiveness, have you come to raise the dead?
Have you come here to play Jesus, to the lepers in your head?'

Now, I am a pretty devout atheist, and the closest I come to religion is watching from a distance. I find religious rituals pretty wasteful. But most disturbing is when people say 'My god is better than your god'. These days one does not hear that as much. It's become more subtle now because people say, 'My spirituality is better than your spirituality'. Or lack thereof, in my case.

But in this particular instance I was quite curious about exactly what happened. How did the visit of the guru help the average prisoner. Was there any lasting spiritual effect?

As a marketing professional I cannot help notice the segmentation that seems to go with gurus, and the parallels between them and brands. Each seems to have his own positioning and appeal. From what I have seen, Sri Sri Ravi Shankar typically appeals to upper- and upper-middle-class devotees. And he has this Amway model of sales and distribution—all for a good cause, of course. Internationally he is probably the biggest Indian name today. So what was he doing in Bokaro Jail? The jail is full of lower class, poor people so his visiting the jail does not seem to fit.

But as I think a little more deeply, it starts to make perfect marketing sense. For a spiritual brand, what better place to get strong PR coverage than a visit to a jail. The target audience in this case is not the people in the jail, but the people who are exposed to the media coverage of the visit to the jail. Cynical me.

So if I take off my marketing hat, what better place for a guru to visit than a jail? A place full of sinners, and people who live a life of crime. Who is more in need of saving and guidance than these people?

So I ask Aseem what he remembers of the visit. He says he, and all the prisoners, remember that the guru came with a lot of women. In an all-male jail full of completely sex-starved young men, and in which one does not even get to see a woman for months, it is not surprising that is the first thing the prisoners would remember. After hearing about the women for a few minutes, I asked him what else happened during the visit. He did not remember too much. He said the guru just spoke for about 10 minutes and left. He remembered just two things. Firstly, the guru had said that, 'You are not a bandi but a bandhu' (You are not a prisoner but a good man). If there was a deeper message Aseem either did not get it or did not remember it. The second thing he remembered was the guru mentioning that he had built a village where there is no crime or theft of any sort. Shops, houses—everything stayed open and unlocked, and things worked entirely on trust. After that Aseem went back to describing the women.

But clearly it was a big event in the jail—well over two years later, people still remembered it. I am hoping there was some other lasting impression. I look in the library to see if—maybe—they had left some Hindi books on the guru's teachings for the prisoners. No such luck.

There were few people who had been in the jail for that long—Nageshwar is one of them. So I ask him about what he remembers. He also immediately recalled the 'Not bandi but bandhu' line. He spoke a little more respectfully about the whole thing. But then he also remembered the women. And the fact that they were not just Indian but also foreign (read 'white') women.

From what I could gather, Sri Sri Ravi Shankar had left a bunch of horny bandhus behind in the Bokaro Jail.

21 January 2013

In the late morning I head towards the library. It is customary for the Zamindar to be sitting at the table in the verandah of the library. Today as I walk past the Zamindar he calls out to me and asks me how things are.

'All is well, thanks to you,' I duly reply.

'Do something to care of us as well sometimes,' he says.

'What can I do to take care of you? You have to take care of us,' I reply, trying to adopt my humblest tone.

He lets it pass, and then enquires about how my case is progressing.

'The hearing is today. Let's see.'

He makes small talk a little longer and in a while says, 'For 26 January we are planning a big event. There will be visitors from outside, lots of food, and entertainment programme by the prisoners etc.'

'Good,' I say in a non-committal tone.

'For this we are taking contributions from all prisoners as well. What would you like to give?' He points to an open register before him. It is the oldest trick in the world: setting the anchor in a negotiation. The register has a list of some prisoner's names—some are blank, and others have amounts written against them: only amounts like 1100 and 2500 rupees etc. No smaller number. Same as the saunf-cum-tip tray that the attendant in a Shatabdi or Rajdhani train proffers at the end of the journey. There are never any small notes or coins visible on that tray—only big ones. And if you put a small one he pockets that, and leaves only the larger ones on display.

'I will give 500,' I said.

'Your position is much above all these others who have given as much as 2500,' he says, with dramatized surprise.

'No such thing. I am not all that rich.'

'Still, 500 is too small an amount for you.' It is being made into a prestige issue.

'Okay 1000, but that is it.'

'It should be at least 2000, but I will not pressure you,' he said, fully cognizant of the fact that I had direct access to his superiors. Later, on speaking to some of the other prisoners I find out that they had all been asked for larger amounts. And the negotiation had been much more one-sided. Basically, they had been told a number. I guess one cannot be in a negotiation with a greater imbalance in the power of the negotiators than this one!

Aseem summed it up beautifully. *'Agar nadi mein rehna hai to magarmuch se dushmani to nahin kar sakte.'* (If you have to live in the river, you cannot be an enemy of the crocodile).

Also, the actual amount becomes 20 per cent higher

because the prisoner has to pay to get the cash into the jail in the first place. I thought this is as blatant as it gets that the authorities were collecting cash from the prisoners when the same authorities were supposed to enforce the rule banning its entry into the jail!

————————

I have a visitor today after three days. Ajay Dubey has come with my bail bond. My release has been secured, and I will finally leave the prison tomorrow if all goes well, or the next day at the latest. That much is certain.

I put my thumbprint on the document in the office, come back to the ward and lie down in my bed just to let it sink in. In a couple of days I will actually, really, be back home with my family. No more nightly lock-up or crappy food or mosquitoes or burping or being in limbo. I actually cannot wait another two days now that it is so real. But more than anything else is an overwhelming sense of relief! No more uncertainty or indefinite waiting.

And as I step outside the ward, preparations for 26 January are in full swing. The juvenile ward kids have been tasked with putting up colourful streamers by sticking colourful paper triangles onto thin jute ropes (*sutali*). And these bright, colourful streamers have been strung across the entire courtyard to dry in the sun. New flowering plants have been planted. Tree trunks have been painted white (with *chuna*) and rust brown (with *geru*). It feels like the whole celebration had been for my release.

But getting a release is a sensitive topic because it is a reminder to everyone else that they are not out yet. I consciously do not talk about it. I would not call it guilt—just awareness of the fact that my joy could be a reminder to others of their pain.

In the ward, Akhilesh has finally been moved out. He had gathered too many non-friends in the ward, I think. He has moved to Ward 1. Best of luck with his praying there.

22 January 2013

Now it's been 29 days in jail. 30 days in captivity. But hopefully I will get out today. However, I did not sleep well last night either. The anger is still there, and I will now have the ability to express it as well.

One of the decisions almost made is that I have to quit Everonn. I don't have another job in hand. I quit once before in my career without having a job in hand, and it turned out to be a bad decision. But I really do not see myself doing even one day's meaningful work for Everonn—I have no faith or conviction left in the company anymore. But I now have to reconcile my desire to quit Everonn with the need to be employed and to have an income. These conflicting thoughts keep me awake half the night.

Anyway, with the morning headcount I start thinking about something to take with me as a souvenir from the Bokaro-Chas Jail. There is this book, of course. But anything else? In the juvenile ward I had seen this seventeen-year-old kid—Kishan Mahto—drawing an excellent pencil-sketch of Subhash Chandra Bose. First I think I would buy that, but then I have an even better idea. Why not ask him if he would sketch a portrait of mine? So I go across and ask him. But he has to go to court, and has other stuff to do. Besides, he is out of paper. He asks if I have a photograph he could sketch from, but I do not. So I dig out a sheet of paper from some legal documents—the backs of which are blank—and ask him again, this time along with some enticements. He finally agrees. We head outside, and I sit in the open on a stool while he sits directly in front of me, and tells me not to move. It is not too difficult except for the flies. He has three different pencils, and is sketching on just ordinary paper. I attempt to sit still for about 90 minutes while he sketches. Of course, the whole project becomes quite the gossip of the jail, so at any given time there would be two or three people looking over Kishan's shoulder—first at the picture and then at me, and back again. There is constant commentary and conversation about the whole process. Poor Kishan, he is probably quite distracted and disturbed.

Anyway, at the end of the 90 minutes I see the portrait and it is quite good. The light and shade for my sweater and scarf is beautifully captured. I feel that he has not done justice to my face, but then I am sure you've heard the statistic that 80 per cent people think they are above average. I am sure that applies to the looks department as well.

When he is done I gift him a small bag of goodies and

some money, and tell him he has done a great job. Considering the circumstances, I genuinely think he has.

———————

So as I am now planning to leave the jail I have to think about people asking for my number, and also whose number I want. Except two people, I don't particularly want anyone's number.

One is Mukur—because I believe he is smart and basically decent, and should get a good break in life. The other is Pappu Ansari.

I take a brief walk with him in the evening today and the conversation turns to rituals and religion. He tells me about how Akhilesh is a good example of lots of religious rituals, and actions to the contrary. I am surprised to hear that, and ask him what he means. He said that his uncle's Scorpio was stolen, and found in Akhilesh's house three days later.

Akhilesh had mentioned to me that the car he is accused of stealing is a white Indica. And, of course, he had claimed to have bought it. But the likelihood of a car being stolen, sold and finally parked in Akhilesh's house within three days is very low in my book. And it still did not explain how a white Indica turned into a black Scorpio. It made me think back to a small question which had popped up in my mind when I had first spoken to Akhilesh about his case. He had said that he already had two cars, and he had bought a third one to ply it as a taxi. I had given him the benefit of doubt—knowing how religious he is, I had just assumed he is not likely to be a car thief. But I actually don't know many school-teachers who own two cars and buy a third one.

I hope the police will eventually establish the facts. But after this new information I am having a serious rethink about whether or not he belongs in the 'innocent/victims' category or the 'criminals' one.

23 January 2013

Still here. There was some delay in some fax reaching the district court. Yesterday I had packed my things up by about 4 p.m., expecting to get out but Nageshwar came and told me that till 2.30 p.m. the release order had not come.

Got a message from my father (through the superintendent and then Aseem) that it might take another day or two.

The coming weekend is a long one: 25, 26 and 27 January are off. If I do not get out by today or tomorrow, I am stuck here for another three days minimum! I want to tell my dad this so that he can pressure the company to make sure it happens.

A prisoner comes looking for me with another bail bond again today at 9.30 a.m. and gets my thumbprint on it.

I tell Aseem I want to meet with the superintendent today to request him to convey the message to my dad. But Aseem says that he had seen my dad in the jail earlier in the morning. That reassured me that they understood the urgency, and he would ensure things would move at the earliest possible.

I do not pack anything, as I am not counting on things to happen. No point hoping for too much and then feeling disheartened. But at 2.30 p.m. the announcement on the PA system says that I needed to come to the gate *with my stuff.*

I go to the gate to ensure I have understood correctly. They confirm that my release order has arrived. I feel like shouting and screaming at the top of my lungs—finally, finally this ridiculous, meaningless ordeal is over. I rush back and pack my stuff. The whole jail has heard the announcement so Pappu Ansari also turns up in my ward to bid me farewell. I only need 10 minutes to pack. I distribute all the packaged food and some toiletries between Raju and Anup. I give the chessboard to Anup. I hope it helps keep his mind busy and occupied.

At the inner gate I hug Pappu and wish him an early exit. Once inside the outer gate area, I go through the release process: it is a two-step process to verify identity— they ask me my name, address and mother's maiden name, and see the identification marks to ensure that some wrong person does not get released. Then a government of India stamp is put on my wrist evidently to ensure that the wrong man is not released. Funny that the only other time I have had my wrist stamped is at a disco. This happens twice, and then we're done. After the whole process is complete, I find Aseem and Nageshwar are also waiting to bid me farewell in the corridor, and I hug them both and thank them. I am ushered into the superintendent's office and meet my father there. We give each other a big hug. He tells me our flight is booked for this very evening. The superintendent keeps talking in his usual, well-meaning but rambling style. But finally, we have to tell him that we have to leave as we have a flight to catch.

And thus I leave Bokaro Chas Mandal Karawas.

The journey to Ranchi and then on to Delhi is uneventful. There is a big reception of friends and family—many with tears in their eyes—waiting for me at Delhi airport. As I step out, my two kids come running towards me, but hesitate as they come closer. The thick beard on my face has them confused.

Within seconds of hearing my voice my son gives me a big hug, and immediately my daughter follows. The two little people cling to me. I see Vandita standing behind them. Unashamed, unabashed tears run down my face. I am home.

Epilogue

28 December 2013

Today, just a year after it all started, I went back to Bokaro Chas jail. Still not sure why. Nostalgia isn't the right word. Neither is 'a walk down memory lane'. Just curiosity, I guess.

I reached the jail and the cops immediately recognized me. I told them I wanted to meet Nageshwar and Aseem—I wasn't sure who else would be there. Part of me hoped the two of them would have been released by now—but they hadn't. I expected the cops to ask me to come into the meeting area. Unexpectedly, I was walked up to the main gate instead.

I wasn't entirely comfortable with that. In fact, for a few moments I was terrified of walking through that gate again. There was no rational argument for this. There was no case anymore. I had come of my own choosing. But still, I felt fear.

However, walk in I did. As I entered both Aseem and Nageshwar were there and visibly happy to see me. We hugged each other. A new jailer had arrived and he asked a ton of questions—in a well-meaning but nosey way. After satisfying him I was escorted to the same meeting room where I used to meet my visitors—my father, Vandita, my brother Vikram and my brother-in-law Vibhuti. Aseem joked that we could meet in 'my office'. The Zamindar was there the whole time, but now he seemed smaller. A lot less intimidating. I guess circumstances change perspectives.

Aseem and Nageshwar both said it was nice of me to come. We made some small talk about how things had changed, how our families were doing, and so on. Then we discussed what had happened to all the people I remembered. Pappu Ansari's case was still on, but he had been released on bail (I had tried to call the number he had given me but it was perpetually switched off). The lawyer who had killed his wife was still in jail. Kishore Bajpai had won his case, and had been released. Ghani hadn't left the jail at all since I had left. Raju had—shockingly—been sentenced to death by hanging. Evidently the girl he was accused of raping and murdering was a minor in her early teens. He had been moved to Hazaribagh Jail, and was appealing the sentencing. Anup had also been released.

Aseem and Nageshwar are, of course, still here. Nageshwar said he had only another 18 months of his sentence, but was requesting for an early release yet again. Aseem's case is still under trial, and his latest request for bail—his fourth in as many years—had been rejected yet again. But he was planning to apply again in a month. As always, he was hopeful.

We ran out of stuff to talk about surprisingly fast. I guess we don't have that much in common, now that I am out. The Zamindar's presence did not help.

———

The eleven months since my release have been really eventful. It took me a few weeks to just come back to normal after my ordeal. Working on this book was also therapeutic in many ways.

Immediately after my release, the first few nights at home were full of nightmares where I wanted to do something but was helpless. I would be at a train station, and could see a train I had to board start moving slowly, but I was unable to move my body, my limbs feeling weighed down. I would be in an open field trying to run and catch other players in some sort of game, but was simply unable to reach anyone at all in spite of my efforts. Same nightmares repeated again and again—in many different versions. I had never had such dreams before.

When I was released, professionally I was in limbo. I had zero motivation to work for Everonn. However, since I was still an accused in a legal case no other employer was willing to touch me with a bargepole. My focus was entirely on ensuring that the case against Everonn (and me) was closed at the earliest. Everonn eventually came through—all parents who had requested a refund were paid. With that done the case had no complainants left and in less than two months of my release the high court quashed the case. Basically, the court said that it was a hollow case, and there was never an intention to commit fraud in the first place. The whole thing felt like a bloody joke at my expense!

I quit Everonn the same month that the case was dismissed and started a new assignment in a few weeks.

As I start to think about what could be the cosmic meaning of my experience, I realize that there isn't any. The lessons for me are simple, and very, very human.

The first is that the world is full of people who may have made grievous mistakes in their lives, but that does not necessarily make them evil. They are still humans, and in many cases very decent human beings. I am not saying they should not be punished for their misdeeds. But they should not all be branded—like they were, at least in my own mind, before my time in jail.

The other interesting learning for me is how religion is practised by different individuals. The difference between an Akhilesh and a Pappu Ansari, to me, is the difference between ritual and the practice of actually living a system of beliefs. In Pappu's case it isn't just Islam, but the religion of 'insaniyat' (humanity). That strongly resonates with me as I consider myself also much more a believer in the faith of 'humanity', which is more important than the act of praying many hours a day and then being an inconsiderate human being, where the ritual becomes more important than actions.

My family had a 'havan' at our house on my return.

About Rs 10,000 was variously burnt, or spent on rich food which was fed to already overfed people. The atmosphere was further polluted, and my carbon footprint went up. I believe using that quantum of money for doing some real good—such as educating a needy child or feeding the hungry—would have earned better 'karma' if there is such a thing. At least a student who received schooling for a year, or a hungry mouth getting a meal, would have given a more genuine blessing than a pundit simply going through the motions ever would.

But the biggest takeaway is the most humbling for me. I really don't think there are special qualities I was born with that set me apart from the crowd in this jail—whether it be the prisoners or the cops. We are all—except for a few rare exceptions—the outcome of our circumstances. I was born into a family where I was well-fed and cared for. I learnt some social skills and good English (I was mostly just an average student) and now I run businesses. My family environment provided well for me, and also taught me the basics well. About the difference between good and bad. About men and women being equal. About being secular. And fair.

At the same stage in their lives, many of the inmates were taught different things by their families and circumstances. Many experienced hunger and malnutrition as children. Many were taught that men were superior to women. That dowry is a one-time lottery ticket. That you should grab whatever you can when nobody is watching.

And many simply weren't taught—with addicted or alcoholic or absent parents, they just had to figure out the world for themselves based on what happened around them. And based on what kind of individual they had formed into, they did things.

The illegality or otherwise of their actions would often be something they would discover only after it was too late. And knowledge of the law would at best be a deterrent, but would not change who they fundamentally were.

Given the number of such people in India, this is a massive problem. And a problem of this stature only has long-term solutions through equitable economic growth and education.

So now, living in the city again, I often hear people talk about the challenges with their low-paid staff or household help. And it is obvious that these educated upper-middle-class people are applying all the paradigms of their own upbringing to everyone else. I can't agree with them or share that perspective anymore. Occasionally—mostly knowing it is futile—I still try and explain. But mostly, I just listen.

The last takeaway is a still-unanswered question. And this is really about the existence of the supernatural. I still don't know what to make of Reiki Chacha. He had pronounced two statements which I needed to verify: one about my brother's knee, and the other about Laddu Gopal being in my 'temple'. I checked both out. Just as Reiki Chacha had said, my brother indeed has a pain in his right knee. But to balance that out, there is no image of Laddu Gopal in the temple in my parents' house. Never was. So the decision is still split.

My faith in not having a faith remains unchanged. And no, I still haven't moved the kitchen stove.

कोचिंग इंस्टीट्यूट पर पुलिस दबिश

एबोन टॉपर्स के स्थानीय निदेशक को ऑफिस से उठा ले गयी

शिक्षकों ने कहा, छात्रों के भविष्य से हो रहा था खिलवाड़

एबोन के पदाधिकारी को थाना ले जाती पुलिस.

संवाददाता ■ बोकारो

सिटी सेंटर के एम-फाइव में चल रहे एबोन टॉपर्स के निदेशक चेतन महाजन को रविवार दोपहर पुलिस उनके ऑफिस से उठा ले गयी. सेक्टर चार थानेदार सुरेंद्र सिंह व सेक्टर छह थानेदार दिनेश कुमार प्रजापति ने सशस्त्र बल के साथ इस कार्रवाई को अंजाम दिया. पुलिस थाने में ले जाकर निदेशक से अभिभावकों को रकम दिलाने के प्रयास में देर रात तक लगी थी, अभिभावकों का आरोप है कि एबोन कोचिंग ने आइआइटी प्रवेश परीक्षा की तैयारी के नाम पर उनसे लाखों रुपये ठगे.

क्या कहा अभिभावकों ने

एबोन भी ब्रिलियेंट व टाइम्स एजुकेशन की तरह कार्यालय बंद कर भागने की तैयारी में है. रविवार देर शाम तक अभिभावकों ने चेतन महाजन से बात कर रास्ता निकालने की कोशिश की. लेकिन बात नहीं बनी. बहरहाल मामले को सुलझाने में पुलिस लगी है. अगर संस्थान ने छात्रों का पैसा नहीं लौटाया तो उक्त कोचिंग संस्थान पर भी जालसाजी कर लाखों रुपये ठगी करने का मामला दर्ज किया जा सकता है.

पहले भी भागे इंस्टीट्यूट

पहले भी बोकारो से रातों रात भागे ब्रिलियेंट कोचिंग, टाइम्स एजुकेशन पर इस तरह का मामला दर्ज किया जा चुका है. लेकिन, उन मामलों में की गिरफ्तार करने में पुलिस को सफलता नहीं मिली है. ठगी के शिकार अभिभावक अब अपने रुपये वापस पाने का ख्वाब भी भूल चुके हैं.

क्या कहते हैं संचालक

चेतन का कहना है उसे कंपनी ने कुछ दिनों पूर्व भेजा है. कोचिंग चालू करने की व्यवस्था हो रही है. दो-तीन दिनों के भीतर संस्थान के मुख्य कार्यालय (रांची) से शिक्षकों को भेजा जा रहा है. इसके बाद कक्षा फिर से चलेगी. लेकिन उनका आश्वासन मानने को अभिभावक तैयार नहीं . वह संस्थान द्वारा लिये गये 70 हजार से एक लाख की राशि वापसी की मांग पर अड़े हैं.

एबोन के छात्र आइआइटियन पेश में कर रहे हैं तैयारी

दूसरी ओर, एबोन छोड़ने वाले शिक्षकों का कहना है : उनके काम छोड़ने से छात्र के भविष्य पर असर नहीं पड़ा है. सभी को अब आइआइटीयन पेश नामक कोचिंग में तैयारी करायी जा रही है. एबोन प्रबंधन छात्रों के भविष्य से खिलवाड़ कर रहा था. इस कारण उन्हें संस्थान छोड़ने पर विवश होना पड़ा. संस्थान में बच्चों को कोई सुविधा नहीं थी. छात्रों की संख्या अधिक व कमरा रूम कम थे. स्टडी मैटेरियल छात्रों को नहीं मिल रहे थे. किताबें भी समय पर मुहैया नहीं किया जा रहा था. किताबें नहीं मिलने से संकाय मासिक आंतर बिजली काट देते थे. इस कारण एक सेशन से लगभग 18 बिन कक्षाएं बाधित रहीं. प्रबंधन ने यहां अपना सेंटर खोला था. यहां वे वेतन भोगी शिक्षक थे.

एजुकेशन हब पर ठगी का ग्रहण !

कुमार शिल्पी व अरविंद ने की शुरुआत

90 के दशक से धंधा

अग्रदूत रहे आरएन सिंह

2001-02 से बंटी कोचिंग

चारू से अचानक दूर धाम

2008 तक एक दर्जन से अधिक संस्थान

11-12 में सबसे अधिक संस्थान खुले

फैकल्टी हाइजैक की हुई शुरुआत

एब्रोन टॉपर्स कोचिंग का प्रबंधक गिरफ्तार

- 500 छात्रों से दो करोड़ से अधिक रुपये लेकर बंद कर दिया था संस्थान
- दो करोड़ से अधिक की ठगी का मामला दर्ज

निज प्रतिनिधि, बोकारो : इंजीनियरिंग एवं मेडिकल की तैयारी के लिए कोचिंग कराने के नाम पर छात्रों का करोड़ों रुपये ठग कर संस्थान बंद करने वाले एब्रोन टॉपर्स के क्षेत्रीय प्रबंधक चेतन महाजन को सेक्टर चार पुलिस ने गिरफ्तार कर चास जेल भेज दिया। पुलिस ने संस्थान के निदेशक राकेश शर्मा पर भी प्राथमिकी की है। दोनों के खिलाफ 200 से अधिक छात्रों

मामले की जानकारी मिली है। इस संबंध में अधिकारियों के साथ बैठक करेंगे। फर्जीवाड़ा करनेवालों के खिलाफ कठोर कार्रवाई की जाएगी।
सुनील कुमार, उपायुक्त, बोकारो

छात्रों की शिकायत पर प्राथमिकी दर्ज हुई है। पुलिस मामले की पड़ताल कर रही है। छात्रों से कोचिंग के लिए पैसा लेकर संस्थान बंद कर दिया गया।
कुलदीप द्विवेदी, एसपी, बोकारो

के हस्ताक्षरयुक्त आवेदन थाने को प्राप्त हुए। अन्य छात्र भी आवेदन दे रहे हैं। छात्रों ने आवेदन में कहा कि संस्थान द्वारा आइआइटी की तैयारी शेष पृष्ठ 17 पर

एब्रोन निदेशक गये

अब जीएम राकेश कुमार शर्मा को गिरफ्तार करने की तैयारी में पुलिस

संवाददाता ■ बोकारो

पिछले एक सप्ताह से छात्रों, अभिभावकों ने पुलिस के चक्कर लगा रहे एब्रोन टॉपर्स (इंजीनियरिंग प्रवेश परीक्षा की तैयारी कराने वाली) कोचिंग के स्थानीय निदेशक चेतन महाजन को चार करोड़ की ठगी के मामले में जेल भेज दिया गया. स्थानीय निदेशक गत पांच दिनों से छात्रों के परिजनों को आश्वासन दे रहे थे कि बंद कक्षाओं को दो-तीन दिनों के भीतर चालू कर दिया जायेगा. एब्रोन के मुख्य कार्यालय (चेन्नई) से शिक्षकों को बुलाया गया है. तीन दिन से अधिक बीत

जेल जाते एब्रोन के निदेशक.

गये पर ना तो फेक्ल्टी आये ना ही बंद कक्षाएं चालू हुई.

85 छात्रों ने संयुक्त रूप से दर्ज करायी एफआइआर : सेक्टर चार पुलिस प्रयास कर रही थी कि छात्रों की पढ़ाई चालू हो जाये या अभिभावकों को

पैसे मिले. अ...
जीएम राकेश...
निदेशक महाज...
ने एफआइआ...
500 छात्रों...
धोखघड़ी कर...
करने का आयो...
...भारका थ... आ...
...श...
कोचिंग में कर...
हुए छात्र धनबा...
भागलपुर आदि...
प्रति छात्र से प...
हजार से लेकर...
गये, लेकिन ना...
चली और ना भ...
गये. पुलिस अब...
कुमार शर्मा ब...
तैयारी कर रही...

Kishan Mahto's sketch of me in Bokaro Jail

ACKNOWLEDGEMENTS

Honestly, this is a first book from a no-name author, and will likely not get anything more than a passing glance from most people. So writing this acknowledgements feels a little like preparing an Oscar speech after having made a home video. But for whatever this book is worth, there were many who have contributed to it coming together, and I want to acknowledge them all.

Firstly, the parents of the students of Everonn Toppers and the Jharkhand police. Their sense of indignation and faulty implementation of the law respectively was the reason I landed up in jail and this book was written. I thank all my fellow inmates, about whom this book essentially is, and who shared their time and stories.

I cannot thank my friends and family enough knowing that they were all working tirelessly, sharing in my agony, and providing strength and support to me in every way possible. My dad was a rock I knew I could depend upon. My wife came through as one of the strongest people I know. Your love provides strength to me always. And everyone who huddled together and called any and every person who they thought could have made a difference. My brother, Cdr. Vikram Mahajan. My brother-in-law, Vibhuti Dubey. Thank you.

Special thanks to Ajay Dubey, a genuinely decent human being who cared immensely about a complete stranger.

I thank Penguin deeply for giving an amateur like me a chance. Specifically, Chiki Sarkar for her clinical, honest and blunt guidelines on what needs to be changed in the book to make it a better read. Paromita Mohanchandra for all her work in the editing. Hussain Zaidi for coming up with a great title.

Last, and most importantly, I thank William Zinnser, for writing the book *On Writing Well*. I picked it up on a whim, and found in it a brilliant guide for every aspect of writing non-fiction. Since I have never met or seen him, in many ways he was the Dronacharya to me, the Eklavya. Thank you.